Political Profiles

# John
# Lewis

John Lewis

# Political Profiles

# John Lewis

Kerrily Sapet

Greensboro, North Carolina

# Political Profiles

Joe Biden

Hillary Clinton

Al Gore

Ted Kennedy

John Lewis

John McCain

Barack Obama

Sarah Palin

Nancy Pelosi

Arnold Schwarzenegger

# Political Profiles: John Lewis

Copyright © 2010 by Morgan Reynolds Publishing

Library of Congress Cataloging-in-Publication Data

Sapet, Kerrily, 1972-
  Political profiles : John Lewis / by Kerrily Sapet. -- 1st ed.
    p. cm.
  Includes bibliographical references and index.
  ISBN 978-1-59935-130-8 (alk. paper)
  1. Lewis, John, 1940 Feb. 21---Juvenile literature. 2. Legislators--
United States--Biography--Juvenile literature. 3. African American
legislators--Biography--Juvenile literature. 4. United States. Congress.
House--Biography--Juvenile literature. 5. Civil rights workers--United
States--Biography--Juvenile literature. 6. Civil rights movements--
Southern States--History--20th century--Juvenile literature. 7. African
Americans--Civil rights--Southern States--History--20th century-
-Juvenile literature. 8. Southern States--Race relations--Juvenile
literature. I. Title.
  E840.8.L43S275 2009
  328.73'092--dc22
  [B]
                                     2009027748

Printed in the United States of America
First Edition

*To Barb, who also helps make the world a brighter place*

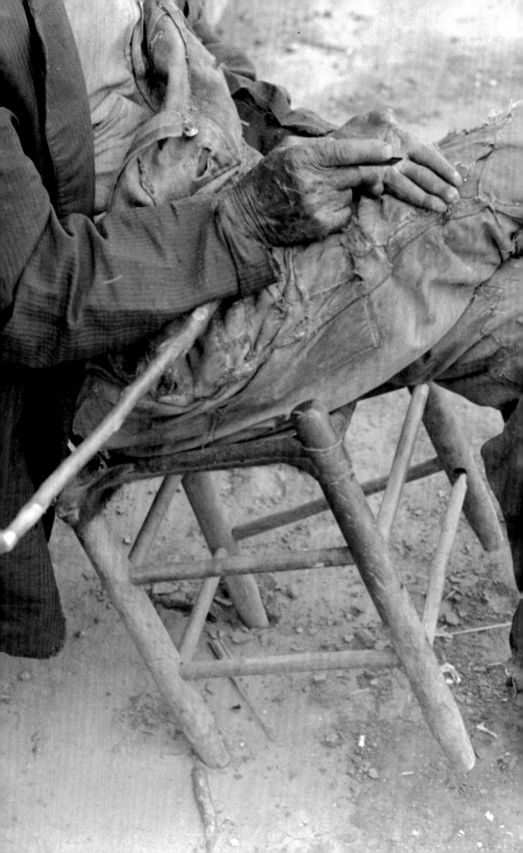

# *Contents*

John Lewis

Chapter *1*
# A Sharecropper's Son

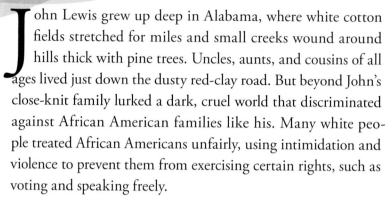

J ohn Lewis grew up deep in Alabama, where white cotton fields stretched for miles and small creeks wound around hills thick with pine trees. Uncles, aunts, and cousins of all ages lived just down the dusty red-clay road. But beyond John's close-knit family lurked a dark, cruel world that discriminated against African American families like his. Many white people treated African Americans unfairly, using intimidation and violence to prevent them from exercising certain rights, such as voting and speaking freely.

As a young boy in the 1940s, John Lewis saw these inequities. As an adult, he dedicated his life to creating a world in which people of all colors would be treated as equals. Lewis led protests, endured beatings, and went to jail to ensure that African Americans were allowed to vote. His efforts and those of fellow activists captured the nation's attention. In 1965, Congress passed the Voting Rights Act. The new legislation removed the voting restrictions that whites had imposed on African Americans in such southern states as Mississippi, Alabama, and Georgia.

In 1986, Lewis reaped the fruits of his efforts, winning election to Congress from Georgia's Fifth Congressional District. He has remained in office ever since, winning reelection ten times. Today, proclaimed *Roll Call* magazine, Lewis reigns as a "moral leader who commands widespread respect in the chamber." On the day that Barack Obama was sworn in as the first African American president, Obama signed a photograph for Lewis. He wrote simply, "Because of you, John. Barack Obama."

John Robert Lewis was born in rural Dunn's Chapel, Alabama, near the town of Troy, on February 21, 1940. His grandmother helped at his birth. John's parents, Eddie and Willie Mae Lewis, had two other children, Ora and Edward. Eventually, John had seven more siblings: Adolph, Sammy, Grant, Freddie, William,

A tenant farmer and young girl work in a field in Eutaw, Alabama, in this 1936 photo.

A sharecropper and his family on the porch
of their North Carolina home in 1939.

Ethel, and Rosa. Sandwiched among the ten children, John was often called Robert, his middle name.

John's family, like most in the area, had ancestors who were slaves. In the mid-1800s, 16,000 of the county's residents were African American, all but ten of them slaves. Although emancipated after the Civil War, African Americans faced fierce discrimination. Laws had changed but attitudes had not. Racism was especially strong in the South, where the plantation system had thrived for so many years. Prejudiced white Southerners passed "Jim Crow" laws that prevented African Americans from having the same education, housing, and employment opportunities as whites. Jim Crow, the name of a black character in a song, was originally a term used to describe a stereotyped image of all African Americans. It eventually became synonymous with segregation in the South.

Without the chance for better schooling and jobs, John's parents, like many African Americans, were tied to the land. They grew up working in the fields. Eddie and Willie Mae met in church in 1932 and married a year later. Shorty and Sugarfoot, as they nicknamed each other, were sharecroppers, like John's grandfather and uncles. As sharecroppers, they rented their farmland from a white landowner. They plowed the fields and planted, tended, and harvested the crops. In return, they received a small portion of the money from the crops' sale.

John's parents scrimped every penny. By the time John was four years old, they had saved up $300 to buy a farm of their own. The family strapped their belongings to their mule-drawn farm wagon and moved a half mile up the road. Their new house was small, but the home and the surrounding 110-acre farm was theirs.

An elderly, black farmer with worn shoes and clothes takes a break from his work, in Green County, Georgia, in 1939. Opposite page: Impoverished tenant farmers, in rural Alabama, circa 1936–1941.

The house had only three rooms, and John shared a bed with two or three of his brothers. Like their neighbors, they had no electricity, heat, or running water. They hauled their water by the bucketful from the well in the front yard.

Behind the house stood a barn where they kept their wagon, farming equipment, and animal feed. They also had a small smokehouse. In prosperous times, meats and sausages hung from its ceiling, along with bunches of hot peppers grown in the family's garden. The family's bathroom, an outhouse, was in the backyard. They used old catalogs for toilet paper in good times, and dried corncobs in bad times. John's mother washed laundry in the backyard, swirling it in a big, black iron pot. In the hot, heavy Alabama summers, they bathed in a small tin tub.

A pecan tree, with nuts so bitter the hogs wouldn't even eat them, shaded the front porch. Wild grapevines tangled the woods around the house. John's family grew food and raised livestock for their own table and to sell. They tended gardens full of peas, corn, peanuts, okra, watermelon, sweet potatoes, and tomatoes. John's mother made peach and blackberry jams, pies, and cobblers. She also made grape juice, which they enjoyed sweet and cold from the icebox. The traveling salesman or "rolling store man" sold supplies the family couldn't grow, such as flour and baking soda, along with treats such as Moon Pies and grape Nehi soda. The rolling store man and the family's old bat-

tery-powered radio were John's only links to the world beyond his family's farm.

"It was a small world, a safe world, filled with family and friends," Lewis remembered. "There was no such thing as a stranger. I never ventured out of the woods of Carter's Quarters—there was no reason and no means. And outsiders rarely ventured in—especially white people."

To make ends meet, everyone worked hard. Although the Lewises farmed their own land, their income had not increased much. John's mother sometimes did laundry or cleaned for white families in Montgomery, Alabama, nearly fifty miles away. John's father drove a school bus. When not working in the family's fields, the older children worked for other farmers. In his spare time, John played with his cousins. They sometimes climbed up on their Aunt Lyzanka's front porch, where she served them bread with syrup.

The Lewises attended church twice a month. On those Sundays, the family piled onto their wagon, the girls wearing their church dresses, the boys wearing their only pairs of slacks and clean, white shirts. The church, with its colorful and energetic services, offered a break from the hard physical labor of their lives. John would always remember the sweet, rich music. It was the sound of people young and old, despite their difficult lives, finding joy by singing together. For John, these songs symbolized freedom and hope.

After church, the Lewis family often went to John's grandparents' house. They all gathered together, eating cheese, tea cakes, and gingerbread. They sometimes had to scrape off mold, as foods didn't keep long in the hot, humid weather.

In 1945, when John was five years old, he started attending school. The school for African American children was just a short walk from his home. The county had separate schools for black and white children. In 1896, the U.S. Supreme Court had ruled in *Plessy v. Ferguson* that segregation was legal, provided that states offered equal facilities for African Americans. This doctrine of separate but equal would last for the next fifty-eight years. Although facilities such as schools were separate, in reality they were not equal. Lawmakers were exclusively white; they built schools only for white children.

John's elementary school was a two-room wooden shack. All of the students and teachers were African American. The school had two teachers and three grades per room. John's school supplies were hand-me-downs from white children. Despite his tattered books, covered with doodles from other children, John loved school from the first day. He especially enjoyed reading. The only book John's parents owned was the Bible. Having the chance to read new stories about famous people and the world beyond Dunn's Chapel thrilled him.

Although John's parents saw that he thrived in school, they needed his help on the farm. During the spring that John turned six years old, he started working in the fields beside his parents and siblings. When there were chores to do, he stayed home to pick cotton, pull corn, or gather peanuts. "This was true for almost every child in our school," Lewis said. "It was a Southern tradition, just part of the way of life, that a black child's school year was dictated by the farm rhythms of planting and harvesting. You went to school when you could."

Although John's family grew many crops, cotton consumed their time, energy, and fields. Picking cotton was backbreaking. He and his family toiled under the hot Alabama sun, often on their hands and knees, planting, fertilizing, and picking the cotton for row after row. John hated the work. To him, it represented

Inside of a dilapidated, overcrowded school for black children in Georgia, 1941

slavery and a lifetime of grueling work with little promise of a better future.

His family stooped in the fields for hours, until their backs felt like they were on fire from the strain. For acres on end, they picked handfuls of cotton, the sharp edges of the pods chewing at their fingers. John's parents earned just thirty-five cents for every one hundred pounds of cotton they picked. Although the family made little money, John's father sometimes handed his children a few coins when they sold their cotton in a nearby town. John loved to buy gingerbread men spread thick with marshmallow cream.

Although John complained about most farm chores, he liked raising chickens. "I fell in love with them," Lewis said. "I named them, talked to them, assigned them to coops and guided them in every night. . . . I also protested when one of them was killed for food. I refused to eat. I guess that was my first protest demonstration."

John thumbed through the Sears Roebuck catalog that was the family's wish book, and longed for an incubator to keep his chicks warm. When any of John's chickens died, he buried them with a funeral service and preached a sermon. His brothers, sisters, and cousins offered flowers and sympathy, and teasingly nicknamed him "Preacher."

A serious child, John stood out from other children because of his keen interest in school and religion. Unlike his siblings and cousins, the farming life frustrated him. His Uncle Otis, the principal of a black school, took interest in his unusual nephew. He saw that John craved a life other than sharecropping. Uncle Otis didn't know what John's future held, but guessed that it would be in the world beyond Troy.

When John was eleven years old, his uncle arranged for him to spend the summer in Buffalo, New York, with relatives. Early one morning in June, John and his mother helped pack Uncle Otis's car for the trip. Not only did they pack John's clothes, but they also filled the car with food. Restaurants in the South didn't serve African Americans. John's mother packed boxes of fried chicken, sandwiches, and sweet potato pie for their trip. Even stopping for gas and to use the bathroom would require caution. Uncle Otis carried a map that marked both safe areas and stops that offered bathrooms for blacks.

John and his uncle made it through Alabama, Tennessee, and Kentucky safely. No longer in the South once they reached Ohio, they relaxed. Vast, blue Lake Erie looked like an ocean to John. He also saw the pounding, misty waters of Niagara Falls. A deeper memory would sink in that summer, though, one that John would carry with him above all others.

John's relatives lived in an integrated neighborhood in

John Lewis, age eleven

Buffalo. John saw black and white people living next door to each other. They ate, shopped, and traveled together. To John, this foreign world was eye opening. By the end of the exciting summer, though, he missed his family and was glad to go home. But home would never seem the same again. John was more aware of the segregation his family faced in the South, and it angered him.

When John returned home, he noticed how blacks and whites were treated differently. Although his father was a grown man, white people often called him "boy." As white people walked by on the streets, African Americans stepped in the gutter to let them pass. Local laws required blacks to use separate water fountains, bathrooms, sections in movie theaters, and more. When an African American bought a Coke, he was handed the bottle and told to drink it outside. For the same price, a white customer could drink the soda in an ice-cold glass, inside the cool store.

That fall, John started junior high school. For the first time, he rode the bus to school. It often arrived late, though, especially when it was rainy. Officials paved roads only in white neighborhoods. Rain made the unpaved clay roads in black neighborhoods slick. The school bus often slid sideways into ditches of thick quagmire. In such cases, the students filed out of the bus and pushed it back onto the road. Sometimes they didn't reach school until noon.

John's parents realized how important school was to their son. But while they wanted him to get an education, they still needed his hands and muscles in the fields. Although John loved school, they insisted he stay home to help during busy times.

Sometimes John hid under the front porch, dressed in his school clothes, to avoid chores. When he heard the bus coming up the road, he made a break for it. Although John's parents were furious when he got home, his father never whipped him.

A segregated bus with white passengers in the front and African Americans in the back.

His parents realized there was no stopping their son once he had made a decision.

At age fourteen, John began attending Pike County Training School. The county had no high school for black students. Instead, the training school taught African American boys to become farmers and laborers, and girls to become maids and housewives.

In 1954, the U.S. Supreme Court made a decision that brought hope to many African Americans like John who longed for better schooling. In the case *Brown v. Board of Education,* the court ruled that segregated schools were unconstitutional, stating that segregation is not equal. For the first time, the U.S. government was condemning segregation. African Americans jubilantly rejoiced.

John figured that his days of shabby schools and old books would end. However, the Supreme Court did not set a timeline for states to desegregate schools. While some states acted, others in the Deep South delayed. Alabama defied the ruling, and schools remained segregated and unequal. Deeply disappointed, John continued to ride the old rattling bus to the segregated school twenty miles away from his home.

For African Americans, there were currents of excitement and fear. A year later, black citizens staged a bus boycott in nearby Montgomery. Rosa Parks, a black seamstress and civil rights activist, was arrested for refusing to give up her seat for a white man standing on the bus. Local laws required African Americans to sit in the back of the bus and give up their seats for white patrons. The black community united in protest. Over the next year, they boycotted the bus service. They walked, car-pooled, and took cabs instead of riding the buses.

The Montgomery Improvement Association, led by Reverend Dr. Martin Luther King Jr., spearheaded the peaceful protest.

Eventually, the U.S. Supreme Court ruled that Alabama state and local bus laws were illegal. On December 21, 1956, African Americans rode desegregated buses for the first time in Montgomery. John, excited to see blacks uniting in protest, avidly read everything he could about the protest. The events in Montgomery changed John's life, unlike any event ever would again. He saw the power of people coming together to peacefully bring about change.

Martin Luther King Jr., the young preacher who led the boycott, became John's hero. King's father and grandfather also were ministers. King had attended Morehouse College in Atlanta, Georgia, and then Boston College in Massachusetts. King offered messages of hope and peace to the growing civil rights movement. His inspiring leadership and nonviolent approaches appealed to many—whether poor, rich, black, white, educated, or non-educated.

Leadership in the African American community often came through the church. During the dark years of slavery, and in the decades that followed, the church was an important force for African Americans. Once a week, the church provided a place free from the insults that black people faced in their lives. Passionate sermons and soaring music fueled people's souls. Many of those songs would become freedom songs, sung to inspire protesters during the civil rights movement.

One day, John listened to a radio program that featured his hero. Reverend King delivered a sermon that linked passages from the Bible to the current racial situation in America. For John, Martin Luther King made religion real. His leadership in the boycott "took the words that I'd heard him preach over the radio and put them into action in a way that set the course of my life from that point on," Lewis later stated.

Martin Luther King Jr.

Other events occurred that shook John. In August 1955, racists in Mississippi murdered fourteen-year-old African American Emmett Till for flirting with a white woman in a store. Despite the two murderers being identified in court, the judge declared them not guilty. Till was just one year younger than John. His murder served as a harsh reminder of the danger all African Americans faced. By the end of the year, John had grown frustrated and angry at the racist system. The inhumanity and injustice gnawed at him, and made him want to take action.

Soon after, Autherine Lucy, an African American woman, tried to enroll at the University of Alabama. She won a court order forcing the school to admit her. Riots ensued. The university's president expelled her, saying it was for her own safety. "Thinking about [her] courage, I became even more convinced that I had to make myself part of all this," Lewis said.

John launched his own small protest. In the spring of 1956, he requested a library card from the local public library, which was for white patrons only. When the librarian refused John's request, he recruited signatures for a petition of complaint. Although he

The jury for the Emmett Till murder trial

Emmett Till

still didn't receive a library card, it was his first step in nonviolent protest.

One year later, John graduated from Pike County Training School. Like his idol, Reverend King, John wanted to study theology. He planned to become a minister. John hoped to attend Morehouse College, where King had gone, but it was too expensive. One day, his mother brought home a pamphlet from an orphanage where she worked part-time doing laundry. It advertised the American Baptist Theological Seminary, a small school in Nashville, Tennessee, for black students who wanted to join the ministry. All of the students worked their way through school, holding on-campus jobs to cover the costs of their tuition, room, and board. John applied, and within weeks the school accepted him.

That fall, John boarded a silver and blue Greyhound bus bound for Nashville. He carried all he owned, his clothing and Bible, in a small trunk. Before John left, his Uncle Otis surprised him with a $100 bill. It was more money than John had ever held before. For years, John had dreamed of the world beyond Dunn's Chapel. When he was little, he and his cousin Della Mae had planned to saw down a towering pine tree near their home and carve it into a bus to leave Alabama. Now John was alone on a bus headed north. It was the start of his new life, although he still had to sit in the back.

Rosa Parks, with Martin Luther King in the background

*Chapter*
# Taking a Stand
**2**

In the fall of 1957, Lewis arrived in Nashville, Tennessee, as the first of his family to attend college. American Baptist Theological Seminary, located on a hilltop overlooking Nashville's skyline, was surrounded by oak trees. A broad field stretched behind its long brick buildings, and the grounds sloped down to the wide brown Cumberland River. Lewis's small dorm room contained two single beds and a pair of battered dressers. To Lewis, who had always slept with a brother or two, it seemed like a palace.

Lewis dove into his coursework, devouring books about philosophy and religion. He enjoyed the whirl of fresh ideas and information, along with the new friendships he quickly made. He washed dishes to pay for his education. At breakfast, lunch, and dinner, Lewis positioned himself in front of a cafeteria sink and scrubbed industrial-sized cast iron pots filled with hot water. Each night, he spent hours scraping off dried food like eggs and liver that was caked to the inside of the heavy pots. Afterwards, the tough sharecropper's son fell into bed, aching and exhausted.

Lewis earned $42.50 each month, $37 of which he paid back to the school for tuition and housing. With the remaining $5.50, he paid for his books and supplies. Money was tight, but life had always been that way for Lewis. In later years at the school, he worked as a janitor, mopping and waxing floors.

Lewis spent time reading all he could about the growing civil rights movement. He tried organizing a student chapter of the National Association for the Advancement of Colored People (NAACP), the organization that had fought and won the *Brown v. Board of Education* case. The NAACP had formed in 1909 to protect blacks from violence and discrimination. The school's president forbade involvement in the NAACP, however, fear-

American Baptist Theological Seminary

ing it would anger the white donors who gave financial support to the school.

Continuing to protest racial injustices, Lewis applied to Troy State College, an all-white school near his home. He hoped to succeed where Autherine Lucy had failed, but his application was ignored. Lewis wrote to the Montgomery Improvement Association, asking for their support in a lawsuit to force the school's integration. Reverend Ralph Abernathy, a close associate of Martin Luther King's, paid for Lewis's bus fare so he could go to Montgomery to speak with Dr. King about his case.

Although Lewis was anxious about meeting his idol, he stated his case well. After consideration, King agreed to support the case against Troy State College, provided that Lewis's parents did, too. King warned Lewis of the harassment he and his family would encounter from angry white protesters. They could lose their jobs and even their lives. Fearful of the repercussions, Lewis's parents couldn't give their son their support. Although disappointed, he understood. It was his fight, not theirs.

Lewis sadly wrote to Dr. King, explaining that he would be returning to school that fall. From Nashville, Lewis read about the exciting civil rights movements sweeping across Africa. Black citizens in African countries, such as Guinea, Zambia, and Ghana, were throwing off the colonial rule of countries like France and Britain. Africans across the continent were fighting for, and winning, their independence.

Although Lewis had been disappointed in his attempts to protest Troy State College's policies, the loss gave him an opportunity. When he returned to college, he began attending a series of church workshops on nonviolent protest. James Lawson, a young African American minister, taught the classes.

As a missionary in India, Lawson had studied the protests of Mohandas Gandhi, an attorney from India. Great Britain had controlled India since the 1700s, instituting many laws that discriminated against the Indian people. Gandhi and his followers disobeyed the laws using peaceful methods, such as marches and boycotts. Great Britain was forced to grant India its independence in 1947. Like Lawson, Dr. King greatly admired Gandhi. The civil rights leaders adopted many of his tactics.

Nonviolent protesters do not fight back. They believe that peace and goodwill are mightier weapons. By not retaliating in the face of attack, they show themselves to be morally superior. Such calm, strong behavior can win supporters to their cause.

Most of the workshops' attendees were college students. They studied philosophy and debated Gandhi's principles. The workshops overshadowed school for Lewis; he believed they were his most important work. They stirred his soul. For him, this work was stronger than church or school. This was the purpose and action he'd been craving since he was a young boy.

At the center of King and Lawson's beliefs was a concept they called the Beloved Community, in which God's kingdom on Earth came together. Members of the community, men and women, had a moral responsibility to struggle nonviolently against forces that prevented harmony in society.

For Lewis, working toward the Beloved Community meant learning how to protest in nonviolent ways. When the students challenged segregation, they would face violence. At the workshops, they practiced curling into

Mohandas "Mahatma" Gandhi

a ball to safeguard their internal organs from punches and kicks. They also learned how to protect each other during physical attacks by using their bodies as shields. Lawson taught them to maintain eye contact with their attackers in an attempt to connect as human beings. At the workshops, they practiced responding to verbal and physical threats. They wanted to be prepared when the time came for action.

The students decided to begin by challenging the segregated lunch counters in Nashville. Many stores had counters where shoppers could order food. Although business owners allowed African Americans to shop in the stores, and gladly took their money, they refused to serve them at the stores' lunch counters. Lewis and the other workshop attendees practiced sit-ins. They planned to force integration by sitting down at lunch counters, peacefully showing their protest. In the workshops, some students acted as the customers. Others acted as racist individuals—jeering, poking, and spitting at the protesters. Lewis helped form the Nashville Student Movement to support the plan.

Students from Fisk University participate in a sit-in in Nashville, Tennessee.

On November 28, 1959, the students held a test sit-in. They walked into a downtown Nashville department store, and each bought an item to establish themselves as paying customers. Next, they sat down at the lunch counter for a bite to eat. When they were refused service, they left. The test sit-in was uneventful, but the students had established the issue. Lewis was excited to have acted.

"All my life I'd heard, seen and obeyed the rules," Lewis wrote. "You can't use that library. You can't drink at that fountain. You can't go in that bathroom. You can't eat in that restaurant. I hated those rules, but I'd always obeyed them. Until now."

Soon the semester ended. When the students returned to school after Christmas, they planned to hold another sit-in. After being refused service, they would sit down and stay seated.

Before Lewis and his fellow students could act, four African American men held a lunch counter sit-in at a store in Greensboro, North Carolina, on February 1, 1960. The protest would spark a wave of sit-ins across the South, although many lunch counters

North Carolina A&T students on the second day of the Woolworth sit-in

simply closed rather than serve African Americans. The students in Nashville were ready.

Jim Lawson held a meeting in which he outlined the plan to stage sit-ins at lunch counters across Nashville. More than five hundred students, both black and white, filled the seats in the auditorium, wanting to join the movement. To Lewis and others, it was important for these new volunteers to understand the concepts of a nonviolent protest. Many students didn't realize that they couldn't fight back. Lewis wrote up a list of guidelines. He told students they needed to avoid aggression. During the sit-ins, they could study, read, write, or talk quietly amongst themselves. They could only get up to use the bathroom, and needed to make sure they had a replacement to fill their seats at the lunch counter. Most importantly, they should be prepared to be arrested and taken to jail.

The group planned its first wave of sit-ins for February 13, 1960. The night before, Lewis could barely sleep from excitement. In the morning, he and more than one hundred other students walked downtown on freshly fallen snow. They split into groups of twenty-five and fanned out to the department stores on Nashville's main street.

Lewis and his group went to Woolworth's. They each bought a small item, and then sat down at the lunch counter on the second floor. The waitress simply stared. A few minutes later, an employee put up a handwritten sign stating that the lunch counter was closed, and then turned out the lights. The students quietly sat at the counter, reading and doing homework. Groups of shoppers stared at them and whispered. A few young white men taunted them, but when the students didn't respond, the men left. When the demonstration ended at 6:00 p.m., the students walked home. Their first true sit-in had gone smoothly.

The students planned more sit-ins over the following days. In each case, the threat of violence loomed. Store managers began to stack blankets, lampshades, and pots on the counter to keep the students from studying.

A white minister heard talk of an attack on the students during the sit-ins planned for February 20. Lewis and the organizers decided to continue. He and his group went to Woolworth's, where they were met by people shouting racial insults.

At lunch counters across the city that day, the students were pushed off their stools, punched, and kicked. Attackers squirted them with mustard and ketchup, poured sugar on them, and held lit cigarettes on their backs. During the violence, the students remained silent, like they had practiced. When the police eventually showed up, they arrested the students. It was the first time Lewis went to jail; he was exhilarated. "It was really happening," he said. "What I'd imagined for so long, the drama of good and evil playing itself out."

Throughout the day, police continued making arrests. More students stepped up to fill the empty stools at the lunch counters. The jailed students opted to remain in jail in protest, rather than pay fines. However, with the jail cells overly packed, police released the eighty-two students.

Nashville's African American residents joined the protest and began to boycott the downtown stores. The students marched in front of the businesses, urging people not to shop there. Their motto was No Fashions for Easter. Many families had traditionally bought new hats, dresses, or shoes for church on Easter Sunday. Instead, the downtown stores remained empty. Some white shoppers stayed away, too.

Early in the morning of April 19, 1960, a group of racists firebombed the home of Z. Alexander Looby, an African American attorney who supported the students. The powerful blast blew out 147 windows of Nashville's main African American hospital one block away. Black and white city residents were shocked and angry. Mayor Ben West denounced the violence. That morning, 5,000 people staged a silent march to City Hall.

"I had never seen anything like the scene as we moved toward city hall that day," Lewis wrote. "The nation had never seen anything like it. This was the first such mass [civil rights] march in the history of America . . . the only sound was the sound of our footsteps, all those feet."

Mayor West met with Diane Nash, Lewis's friend who led the march, on the steps of city hall. Lewis listened as Nash asked the mayor to help end racial discrimination. She asked him if he would recommend that the lunch counters be desegregated. The mayor said "yes," then mumbled that the decision was up to store owners. Everyone simply heard the word "yes." The *Tennessean* ran a front-page headline stating the mayor wanted the lunch counters integrated. On May 10, 1960, African Americans were served at lunch counters throughout downtown Nashville for the first time.

That same spring, local leaders of student protests gathered in Raleigh, North Carolina, to discuss the movement. At the meeting, Lewis helped form the Student Nonviolent Coordinating Committee (SNCC). The group, which would be at the forefront of many civil rights protests, would play a large role in Lewis's life.

Lewis began to travel and speak to other college groups about nonviolent protest. That fall, his group expanded its sit-ins to include restaurants beyond the downtown area as well as segregated hotels, grocery stores, and fast food places. They also targeted movie theaters.

African Americans were required to sit in the balcony at theaters. They paid for their movie tickets, then walked outside into dark alleys and climbed up rickety metal fire escapes to get to the balcony. The students staged stand-ins to protest this segregation. They waited in ticket lines to request a non-balcony ticket at the window. When they were refused, they returned to the end of the line to repeat the process.

Often white hoodlums pelted the students with eggs, rocks, snowballs, and stink bombs. If police did step in, they arrested the protesters, not the attackers. Violence didn't deter the students, even if it sometimes left them hospitalized. The attackers also abused newspaper reporters, smashing their cameras to prevent them from exposing the violence.

Some white protesters, including Jim Zwerg, took part in the sit-ins and stand-ins. They often were singled out for special abuse from racist groups. Zwerg and Lewis met in Nashville. Both students were similar in age, but they had grown up in different worlds. However, they stood together to end segregation. Attackers beat Zwerg with wrenches and iron pipes as he tried to help desegregate the theaters.

On February 20, 1961, Lewis was arrested during a stand-in. Now a senior in college, he turned twenty-one years old in prison the next day. "Growing up in the rural South, it was not the thing to do . . . to go to jail," Lewis said. "I would bring shame and disgrace on the family. Me, I'll tell you, it was like being involved in a holy crusade. It became a badge of honor." Lewis's parents were horrified.

Eventually, the Nashville movie theaters relented and agreed to desegregate. Zwerg taped the ticket stub from that first movie in his journal, calling it the best show he'd ever seen. Lewis would rarely go to the movies, though; memories of sitting in the balcony remained too strong.

That spring marked the end of Lewis's time at American Baptist Theological Seminary. After graduation, he wanted to continue working for the civil rights movement. Much to his parents' dismay, he had also decided against becoming a minister.

"I lost my family that spring . . .," Lewis said. His mother told him: "You went to school to get an education. You should get out of this movement, just get out of that mess."

Determined to continue building a better community, Lewis applied for a job with the American Friends Service Committee, to help construct homes in Africa or India. But then he saw an ad from the Congress of Racial Equity (CORE) group. They were seeking volunteers to test the desegregation of interstate buses in the South. They called it the Freedom Ride. Lewis wrote for an application. When it arrived, it cautioned volunteers of the extreme danger and violence they would face. Lewis was undeterred.

"At this time," Lewis wrote on his application, "human dignity is the most important thing in my life. This is the most important decision in my life, to decide to give up all if necessary for the Freedom Ride, that Justice and Freedom might come to the Deep South."

Lewis soon received a response from CORE. Contained within was an acceptance letter and a one-way ticket to the training workshop in Washington, D.C. It was the sweetest graduation present Lewis could have imagined.

43

B y 1960, African Americans had been challenging segregated transportation for years. As far back as the 1800s, Sojourner Truth and Frederick Douglass had refused to give up their seats on trains to white passengers. In one instance, Douglass clung to the "whites-only" seat until it tore loose from the floor. In 1955, Rosa Parks would not yield her seat on a bus. The time was ripe for another challenge.

The U.S. Supreme Court had outlawed segregated seating on interstate bus travel back in 1946. The Congress of Racial Equity (CORE) tested some states' compliance by taking a bus trip through the South. Over the next two weeks, fifteen of the sixteen riders were beaten, twelve of them were arrested, and eight of them were sentenced to jail time. States continued to ignore the Supreme Court's decision for many more years. Most laws in southern states required black passengers to sit in the back. Bus terminals still had separate waiting rooms, restrooms, restaurants, and drinking fountains for black patrons.

In 1960, the Supreme Court extended its ruling to desegregate the facilities in bus depots that served passengers traveling between states. According to the ruling in *Boynton v. Virginia*, once a bus crossed state lines, it was subject to federal, not state, laws. Passengers journeying across state lines could sit where they wanted and use any facilities in the terminals.

After states defied the ruling, civil rights leaders planned a bus trip they called the Freedom Ride. They hoped to illustrate the continued segregation and provoke the federal government into enforcing the law. CORE chose thirteen volunteers, a mix of black and white, as the Freedom Riders. At age twenty-one, John Lewis was the youngest.

In the spring of 1961, each of the Freedom Riders traveled to Washington, D.C., for three days of training in nonviolent resistance. They practiced remaining calm when verbally and physically abused, and letting their bodies go limp when attacked. Over a period of thirteen days, the Freedom Riders would journey through seven segregated states, stopping at terminals in Virginia, North Carolina, South Carolina, Georgia, Alabama, Mississippi, and Louisiana. They would cover about 1,500 miles of highway in the South.

On May 3, the night before they left, the volunteers dined together in an elegant Chinese restaurant. Waiters served the Chinese food—something Lewis had never eaten before—on shining silver platters. Despite the delicious food and new friendships, the mood was serious. The Freedom Riders would be risking their lives to expose the injustice of the traditions and laws that treated African Americans unfairly. Several of them

Protesters display signs during a Freedom Ride.

wrote out wills. Lewis didn't, though; he had no possessions to leave his family.

On March 4, 1961, the Freedom Riders left Washington. They boarded a bus that crossed the Potomac River and headed out into the rolling Virginia farmland. At their stops in Virginia, the "White Only" and "Colored Only" signs had been taken down in the terminals. The riders only attracted stares. They also safely traveled through North Carolina.

On May 9, 1961, they arrived in Rock Hill, South Carolina. Lewis had shared a front seat with fellow Freedom Rider Albert Bigelow, a white man. When they got off the bus, Lewis headed to the "white" waiting room and Bigelow to the "colored" waiting room. Two white teenagers lurked at the entrance to the waiting rooms. They blocked Lewis's path and attacked him. Bigelow tried to protect Lewis by shielding him with his body, but the teens beat Lewis badly. Police in the terminal watched the assault and finally ended it. Lewis's years of training as a nonviolent protester had taught him not to be angry with the teens who battered him. The Freedom Riders weren't battling against one person, but instead the entire system that created racist people.

The attack produced the effect that the Freedom Riders had desired. It drew attention to their cause. But while reporters covered the events in Rock Hill, the story was overshadowed by the news of astronaut Alan Shepard, the first American to journey into space.

Lewis reluctantly left the Freedom Rides for a few days for a job interview with the American Friends Service Committee. He flew to Philadelphia and met with the committee. Two days later they offered him a post in India, starting in the summer, which he accepted. He also made plans to rejoin the Freedom Riders in

Alabama. The volunteers had continued their ride through South Carolina and Georgia, into the heart of the South.

On May 13, the Freedom Riders met for dinner with Martin Luther King in Atlanta. They toasted the fact that seven hundred miles of the journey were behind them. King pulled aside a reporter from *Jet* magazine traveling with the riders and whispered, "You will never make it through Alabama."

Alabama was called the Heart of Dixie, and segregation ran deep. Signs emblazoned with the emblem of the Ku Klux Klan welcomed travelers to towns and cities.

The Klan had thrived in the South since the end of the Civil War. Its name originated from the Greek word *kuklos*, meaning "circle." Prejudiced whites, angered by new freedoms granted to emancipated slaves, terrorized African Americans. Draping themselves in white gowns and tall pointed hats that masked their faces, they raided homes, beating and murdering black citizens. The Ku Klux Klan quickly spread throughout the South, and it remained active in the 1960s. Klan members, many of whom held positions as civil leaders and police officers, were determined to protect their segregated way of life. The Freedom Riders were a prime target.

On Sunday, May 14, the Freedom Riders divided into two groups. To test different bus companies, nine of the volunteers took a Greyhound bus and the others boarded a Trailways bus. The buses would stop at the terminal in Anniston, Alabama, before heading on to Birmingham.

The Greyhound bus reached Anniston first and pulled into the terminal. An armed mob was waiting. They slashed the bus's back tires before the driver sped off. Fifty cars and pickup trucks followed the wounded bus. When it broke down six miles later, two hundred people attacked. They smashed the windows and

A Greyhound bus goes up in flames after an angry mob near Anniston, Alabama, set it on fire.

tossed a firebomb inside the bus. The Freedom Riders escaped just before the bus's fuel tank exploded. The angry crowd pelted them with rocks and bricks. By the time Alabama state troopers arrived, the mob had done its damage. All of the Freedom Riders suffered from injuries and smoke inhalation. Lewis heard about the tragedy on the radio and was stunned. The next morning, newspapers across the country ran photographs of the smoking bus.

The Trailways bus carrying the other Freedom Riders also met disaster. It pulled into Anniston shortly after the first bus. At the terminal, men climbed on board and dragged the Freedom Riders to the back of the bus. Armed with clubs and bottles, they beat the riders as the bus sped toward Birmingham.

When the bus pulled into Birmingham, a mob was waiting. Local police let them attack for fifteen minutes before they intervened. People in the crowd kicked Freedom Rider Walter Bergman, a sixty-year-old white professor, repeatedly in the head. He sustained brain damage and was paralyzed for life. Freedom Rider Jim Peck ended up with a mouthful of broken teeth and head wounds so deep that they required fifty-three stitches to close. The mob abused reporters and smashed their cameras.

The violence in Alabama made national news, bringing attention to the Freedom Riders and their cause. People questioned why the Birmingham police had not stepped in sooner. Eugene "Bull" Connor, the police chief, retorted that he had given many of his officers the day off for Mother's Day. Years later, officials admitted that they had intentionally allowed local Klan members to attack. Many white Southerners had resented the "meddling" of the "outside agitators."

"Every decent Southerner deplores violence," said George Huddleston Jr., a congressman from Alabama. "But these trespassers—these self-appointed merchants of racial hatred [the Freedom Riders]—got just what they deserved."

The violence shattered the Freedom Ride. The riders who weren't hospitalized decided that the Freedom Ride was too dangerous to continue. Back in Nashville, Lewis and the Student Nonviolent Coordinating Committee (SNCC) decided to keep the Freedom Ride going. "If not us, then who?" Lewis said. "If not now, then when? Will there be a better day for it tomorrow or next year? Will it be less dangerous then? Will someone else's children have to risk their lives instead of us risking ours?"

They chose ten volunteers to continue the ride. John Lewis was the only person to begin and end the Freedom Ride. His friend Jim Zwerg also volunteered. Many of the students wrote wills and said final goodbyes to their family and friends, not knowing if they would return.

From Nashville, Diane Nash helped coordinate the ride. Afraid that her phones were tapped, she told civil rights workers in Birmingham to expect a shipment of "chickens" the next day, a code word for the Freedom Riders. On the bus to Alabama, Lewis recalled his trip with Uncle Otis as a child. They had packed food because restaurants wouldn't serve them. They were also turned away from restrooms, and forced to use the side of the road. Lewis hoped the Freedom Ride would help end those humiliations.

On May 17, 1960, the ten "chickens" arrived at the terminal in Birmingham. Bull Connor was ready. He arrested them, saying it was for their own safety. For two days, the police held the riders in jail. Then they loaded them onto a truck at midnight and stranded them on the border of Alabama and Tennessee. The students feared that the police had set them up to be murdered by Klansmen.

The riders tramped through the countryside under the moonlight. Near dawn, an elderly African American couple risked their lives by taking the Freedom Riders into their home. They gave them warm water to wash and bought them bread, bologna, and cheese—the first food the students had eaten in two days. Lewis telephoned Nash, who sent a car to rescue them.

Determined to succeed, the Freedom Riders returned to Birmingham, along with eleven other "chickens" who had been shipped. The twenty-one Freedom Riders united in Birmingham and planned to take the bus to Montgomery. They had the nation's attention. After hours of furious debate, Robert Kennedy, the attorney general and President John F. Kennedy's brother, forced the Alabama governor to guarantee the safety of the riders. Even so, it would be a new battle in every town.

The bus pulled out of the terminal and headed for Montgomery, with just the Freedom Riders inside. Police cars with flashing lights and screaming sirens escorted the bus to the city limits. From there, the Alabama highway patrol flanked the bus and police airplanes flew overhead. Just outside of Montgomery, the police protection disappeared. The riders arrived at an eerily quiet station. As they disembarked, Lewis stopped and stared. A mob of 1,000 people was waiting.

The angry crowd of men, women, and children wielded chains, baseball bats, tire irons, and rubber hoses. Even the reporters' cameras became weapons. Lewis tried to help the Freedom Riders escape to a nearby church, but attackers bashed him over the head with a wooden crate. His knees buckled, everything went black, and blood streamed from his head.

A few of the Freedom Riders escaped. The mob continued to beat the remaining students until Floyd Mann, a public safety director, fired into the air to disperse the attackers. He pulled the men off the Freedom Riders, saving their lives. Lewis was taken to an African American doctor, who bandaged his head. Zwerg, who had nearly been killed, gave a press conference from the hospital. He told reporters he would accept death in order to get to New Orleans and complete the ride.

Although Alabama's attorney general issued a court injunction ordering the Freedom Ride to stop, Lewis and others argued that the Freedom Ride was not breaking any laws. Within four days, the injunction was lifted. Heavily bandaged, John Lewis—along with the other Freedom Riders and Martin Luther King—declared that the Freedom Ride would continue.

On May 24, 1961, twenty-seven Freedom Riders boarded buses bound for Jackson, Mississippi. Before leaving, most of them stuffed notes in their pockets to identify themselves if they were injured or killed. The buses passed through Mississippi with a police convoy more than a mile long. Helicopters and planes flew overhead; soldiers with bayonets on their rifles stood on the bus to protect the Freedom Riders.

At the Jackson bus terminal, police arrested Lewis for trespassing in the "white" restroom. They arrested the other Freedom Riders, as well. A judge sentenced them to six weeks in prison. For two weeks, police held them in the county jail. One night, the guards

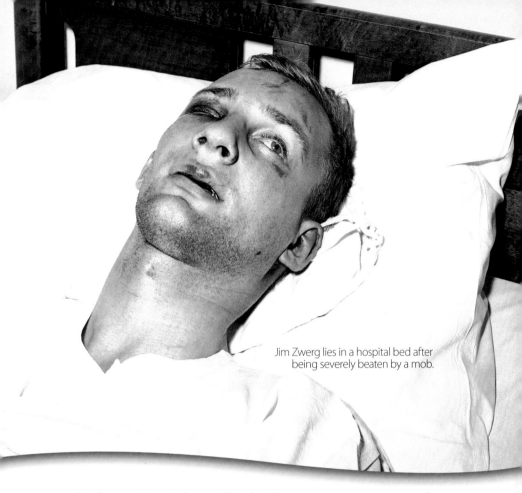

Jim Zwerg lies in a hospital bed after being severely beaten by a mob.

woke the Freedom Riders and herded them, at gunpoint, into truck trailers. After a two-hour drive, they stopped in the country at a jail surrounded by miles of barbed wire. They had become prisoners at Mississippi's infamous Parchman State Penitentiary.

"We were forced to strip naked and wait for an hour and a half, without knowing what was going to happen to us," Lewis said. "For the first time in my life, I was literally . . . terrified."

Guards placed the students in cells, providing each of them with only an undershirt and a pair of shorts. The guards were not allowed to touch the Freedom Riders, by order of the Mississippi governor who wanted to avoid bad publicity. It didn't stop them from terrorizing the students, though. The guards blasted them with fire hoses, and then turned on giant fans to freeze them. They used cattle prods on the students and placed them in restraints nicknamed wrist-breakers, devices that progressively tighten around the wrists.

From jail, Lewis wrote to the American Friends Service Committee to cancel his assignment in India. He wanted to continue working for freedom in his own country. The students sang freedom songs to keep their spirits up, even though the guards took their mattresses away in retaliation.

"We used to rock the jails [at Parchman]," Lewis said. "The [criminals] prisoners downstairs used to sing with us."

While Lewis and the other Freedom Riders served their jail sentences, a new crowd of Freedom Riders rose up to take their places. The newspaper reports and images of violence on the nightly news had inspired other courageous volunteers. More than 1,000 people made Freedom Rides that spring and summer. Soon, hundreds filled Mississippi's jails. Lewis stated:

*There was a spirit within us that would not die. The forces of hatred and violence tried to burn it out of us in Anniston. They tried to beat it out of us in Montgomery. They tried to jail it out of us through the cold and lonely humiliations of Parchman Penitentiary in Mississippi, but nothing could destroy our commitment to see the Freedom Rides through.*

On July 7, the prisoners were released. New Freedom Riders continued to flood the South. On September 22, 1961, the Freedom Riders realized their goal when the Interstate Commerce Commission (ICC) issued regulations that gave teeth to the Supreme Court's ruling. The law required terminals to post signs stating that seating on buses took place without regard to race, color, creed, or nationality. Bus companies that sent vehicles to segregated states would be breaking the law.

Within three months, several teams of CORE riders tested the changes with success. By the end of 1962, after eighty-five rides

through public transportation terminals in the South, they declared the battle won. The Freedom Ride marked a change in the racial war. It motivated thousands of people—children, teens, and adults—to join the civil rights movement. However, it also escalated tempers and prompted fiercer resistance.

Although Lewis had helped achieve great things, his involvement as a Freedom Rider further alienated him from his family. He recalled:

*[They] never understood why I had become involved. They thought I was just going bad. . . . I did go back to Alabama to see my folks for a few days later that summer, but I needed contact with people who understood and supported me. . . . The movement . . . became my family.*

To many, Lewis and the nine students who had continued the Freedom Ride were heroes. Martin Luther King's organization, the Southern Christian Leadership Conference (SCLC), formed by black leaders to organize nonviolent protests, praised the students. The group awarded each of them $500 scholarships and presented them with the Freedom Award. King told Lewis how important he had been to the movement. With his scholarship money, Lewis decided to pursue a degree in philosophy at Fisk University. However, he took a light course load, which allowed him time to continue his civil rights work.

By 1962, John Lewis was no longer a quiet boy from the country. The sit-ins, the protests, and the Freedom Ride had given him confidence and determination. At only twenty-two years old, he had become an influential leader in the civil rights movement.

*Chapter*

# 4

# Freedom Summer

In 1963, Birmingham, Alabama, held the title of the South's most segregated city. From inside the city's restaurants, theaters, hotels, elevators, and restrooms to outside in its parks and pools, black and white people lived, played, and prayed separately. Alabama's new governor, George Wallace, authorized violence and delivered fiery speeches to protect this segregated way of life. "In the name of the greatest people that ever trod this earth, I draw the line in the dust and toss the gauntlet before the feet of tyranny," Wallace said. "And I say: Segregation now! Segregation tomorrow! Segregation forever!"

In April 1963, civil rights leaders zeroed in on Birmingham. They organized thousands of people to take part in sit-ins and boycotts. Teenagers and children staged demonstrations, too. During one rally, police officers arrested nearly one thousand black children. The city's outraged black residents demanded

Downtown Birmingham in 1963

Birmingham police and fire fighters use police dogs and water hoses to break up young protesters.

their release. Police chief Bull Connor complied, promising no more arrests. Instead, when the children marched again, he unleashed snarling German shepherds and used fire hoses with jet streams strong enough to peel the bark off a tree. The pictures on the evening news horrified Americans and people around the world. They left a lasting impression.

Like other Americans, President John F. Kennedy saw the images of the attacks on Birmingham's children. On June 11, he appeared on national television and announced his intention to send a sweeping civil rights bill to Congress. Kennedy said:

John F. Kennedy

*We are confronted primarily with a moral issue. . . . The heart of the question is whether all Americans are afforded equal rights and equal opportunities, whether we are going to treat our fellow Americans as we want to be treated. . . . [O]ne hundred years of delay have passed since President Lincoln freed the slaves, yet their heirs, their grandsons are not fully free. . . . And this nation, for all its hopes and all its boasts, will not be fully free until all of its citizens are free. Now the time has come for this nation to fulfill its promise.*

Throughout the empty promises, protests, and violence of early 1963, Lewis bravely continued his fight. His colleagues respected his dogged determination and commitment to non-violent resistance. In June, they elected him chairman of SNCC.

Lewis dropped out of Fisk University, a few credits shy of his degree. He packed up his few belongings and moved to Atlanta, SNCC's headquarters. For the first time, he had a place of his own, without family, roommates, or prison cellmates.

As SNCC's chairman, Lewis traveled, visited ongoing projects, gave speeches, and spoke with reporters. When Martin Luther King announced plans for a huge march in Washington, D.C., in August, Lewis helped make it happen. The March on Washington for Jobs and Freedom would become the largest demonstration in American history.

As a top civil rights organizer, Lewis would speak at the march. As the day approached, he worked with advisors to write his speech. Other speakers decided his words were too forceful. Lewis compromised and revised his speech.

On August 28, people flocked to Washington. They journeyed by bus, train, plane, and foot. They crowded the Mall

IN THIS TEMPLE
AS IN THE HEARTS OF THE PEOPLE
FOR WHOM HE SAVED THE UNION
THE MEMORY OF ABRAHAM LINCOLN
IS ENSHRINED FOREVER

March organizers gather at the Lincoln Memorial after the March on Washington. From left to right: Matthew Ahmann, Cleveland Robinson, Rabbi Joachim Prinz, A. Philip Randolph, Joseph Rauh Jr., John Lewis, and Floyd McKissick.

in front of the Lincoln Memorial. Such famous Americans as baseball player Jackie Robinson, actor Sidney Poitier, and singer Bob Dylan attended. An estimated 250,000 people, of all races, united in Washington to call for racial justice.

When Lewis stood up on the steps of the Lincoln Memorial to deliver his speech, the sight of so many people awed him. His voice nearly failed, but he found the courage to continue. Lewis told the crowd:

> *By the force of our demands, our determination and our numbers, we shall splinter the desegregated South into a thousand pieces and put them back together in the image of God and democracy. We must say, 'Wake up, America. Wake up!" For we cannot stop and we will not be patient.*

Many considered Lewis's speech the fieriest of the day. Martin Luther King's speech, though, was the most memorable. It stirred the hot, tired crowd, and became his most famous.

> *I have a dream," King said, "that my four little children will one day live in a nation where they will not be judged by the color of their skin but by the content of their character.*

King described black and white people becoming friends, and freedom ringing out for all citizens. His inspiring words captured the hope Americans wanted to feel. At the end of the day, they

A quarter of a million Americans packed the Mall on August 28, 1963, for the March on Washington for Jobs and Freedom.

carried his message home with them, dreaming of a new nation where all people were treated fairly.

A few days later, however, a tragedy occurred that shook people's optimism. On September 15, a bomb went off at a black Baptist church in Birmingham, killing four girls and injuring more than twenty other churchgoers. Although Alabama police arrested the three men responsible for the bombing, they charged them only with illegally possessing dynamite, not with murder.

The church bombing delivered a blow to those who believed change would come. Many people new to the civil rights movement didn't understand the principles of nonviolent resistance. Many of them did not want to. Lewis worried that the civil rights movement was taking a radical and violent turn.

Robert Williams, an NAACP chairman from North Carolina, advocated violence and retaliation. Malcolm X of the Nation of Islam represented black nationalism, a movement much different than Lewis's interracial democracy. He advocated for an all-black movement, and also urged blacks to fight back "by any means necessary." These words appealed to many African Americans, who had been frustrated for so long. Others, though, both in the movement and beyond, found this wave of anger alarming.

Although white brutality against blacks sickened President Kennedy, he was concerned about the increasingly violent tone of the civil rights movement. He suggested that the movement's leaders focus on less contentious issues, such as voting rights. If African Americans were allowed to vote, they could bring about long-term change.

After much debate about the direction of the civil rights movement, SNCC leaders agreed to focus on voting rights. However, President Kennedy and civil rights workers soon learned that

A view of the damage caused by the bomb that exploded outside the Sixteenth Street Baptist Church in Birmingham. The explosion killed four black girls attending Sunday school.

registering voters was an explosive issue. Fierce segregationists saw no difference between direct action and voter registration.

The population of African Americans was greatest in the South. Many white Southerners feared that if African Americans could vote, they would vote white officials out of office. According to the U.S. Constitution's Fifteenth Amendment, passed in 1870, denying people the right to vote based on race was illegal. However, many southern states circumvented the law.

They employed many tactics to prevent African Americans from voting. Officials charged poll taxes, or fees, to vote, and they required black voters to take "literacy" tests (or civics tests) that many of them could not pass. White voters weren't subjected to the same requirements. Officials also mandated that voters apply in person at the courthouse for registration, which was open just a few hours each month. Often African Americans worked during those hours, or had no transportation to the courthouse. Counties also published voters' names. Black voters were often fired from their jobs and evicted from their homes for registering. In 1961, Herbert Lee, an African American farmer from Mississippi, was killed for urging blacks to register.

In 1961, only 5 percent of Mississippi's eligible black voters were registered. Statistics in Alabama were equally grim. In the county surrounding Selma, only two hundred of the 15,000 eligible black voters were registered.

Using the slogan One man, One vote, SNCC workers organized voter registration drives in Selma. On Freedom Mondays, hundreds of African Americans lined up at the courthouse to register. State troopers and angry posses harassed and beat them. The police frequently arrested Lewis and the protesters. Using electric cattle prods, they herded them onto buses, then confined them in filthy chicken coops.

When officials in Mississippi prevented African Americans from voting in a primary election, civil rights workers held a Freedom Vote on Election Day in 1963. To give black Mississippians the experience of voting, they placed ballot boxes in barbershops, beauty parlors, stores, and churches. Although only a mock election, the voters faced fierce opposition. By the day's end, more than one hundred incidents of police interference had occurred. However, 90,000 African Americans had voted.

Political Profile: **John Lewis**

On November 22, 1963, gunman Lee Harvey Oswald assassinated President Kennedy in Dallas, Texas. The world mourned. "Kennedy represented hope and possibility to most of America, white and black alike," Lewis stated, "and when he died, that flame of optimism in all of us flickered just a little bit lower."

Vice President Lyndon Baines Johnson was sworn in as president immediately upon Kennedy's assassination. He was a white Southerner from Texas. Civil rights activists wondered how Kennedy's death would affect their cause. However, one of President Johnson's first acts was to urge Congress to pass Kennedy's proposed civil rights legislation, as a memorial to the slain president.

In 1964, Lewis and other civil rights activists continued their fight for voting rights. With the presidential election in November, they hoped to build upon the success of the Freedom Vote. They began to plan a massive operation to register Mississippi's black voters and to challenge illegal practices within political parties. They called the project Freedom Summer. Bob Moses headed the Freedom Summer project, and members of the Council of Federated Organizations (COFO) undertook the dangerous work. COFO was comprised of several civil rights organizations, including the NAACP, CORE, SCLC, and Lewis's SNCC, which was the dominant group.

The Mississippi Democratic Party had recently chosen its delegates for the Democratic National Convention in August. However, they had excluded black voters registered as Democrats from participating in the delegate selection process. As an alternative to the discriminatory practices of the Democratic Party, civil rights leaders formed their own party, the Mississippi Freedom Democratic Party (MFDP). They hoped to enlist enough support during Freedom Summer to make their voices heard during the presidential election.

COFO recruited hundreds of white college students to help, hoping they would draw attention to the cause. The volunteers would talk to prospective voters, drive them to the courthouse to register, and teach classes in Freedom Schools that, in part, would prepare them for the literacy tests. COFO amassed approximately eight hundred volunteers, the majority of them white.

COFO established its headquarters in Hattiesburg, Mississippi, in the heart of the violence. An armed guard protected their offices. Officials in Mississippi prepared, too. Local police departments stockpiled weapons, tear gas,

Lyndon Baines Johnson signs the Civil Rights Act of 1964.

and guns. The city of Jackson bought a tank with a submachine gun. In one night, the Ku Klux Klan burned crosses in sixty-four of the state's eighty-two counties. The fiery crosses symbolized the terror and dominance of the Klan.

The volunteers gathered in the small college town of Oxford, Ohio, for training. SNCC workers prepared them for the hostility and assault they would face. After training, they headed south to Mississippi.

In an article dated June 21, 1964, a *New York Times* reporter wrote:

> . . . . *[volunteers] will face white hostility in all the smallest cities, dusty county seats, farms and plantations of the countryside. They will attempt in two months to bring a lasting change in the pattern of segregation under which Negroes have lived for a century. No one can predict the outcome.*

The day those words were published, three of the volunteers disappeared just hours after they arrived in Mississippi. Mickey Schwerner, Andy Goodman, and James Chaney had been inspecting the remains of a burned Freedom School. Wanting to keep close tabs on their volunteers for safety reasons, COFO had strict rules about check-in times. When the three men failed to show up on time, they grew concerned.

A local sheriff admitted to arresting the men for speeding, but said he released them after they paid a fine. However, the volunteers had not phoned COFO upon their release. No one saw them alive again.

The volunteers' blue station wagon, which had been burned, was found in the swampy, snake-infested waters of a nearby creek. Lewis and thirty-five other civil rights leaders swarmed

SCHWERNER      CHANEY      GOODMAN

Mississippi, demanding to see the Freedom School and the car. Police refused, telling them that both were on private property. Lewis and others searched the area secretly that night, but found no clues. Soon President Johnson ordered 150 FBI agents and Navy sailors in nearby Meridian, Mississippi, to join the efforts.

As the hunt for the three volunteers continued, the U.S. Congress passed President Kennedy's Civil Rights Bill. The law made segregation in public places and discriminatory hiring practices illegal. Little changed, though, in Mississippi that summer. COFO volunteers continued their work, and danger loomed day and night. Leery of being alone, they traveled in groups for safety.

To be less conspicuous, they often drove at night, rocketing down dark dirt roads, wary of headlights in their rearview mirrors. Black volunteers who opened up their homes to house the workers also faced grave danger. Bullet holes scarred the front door of one Freedom House. Inside, the besieged volunteers found comfort and friendship. They stayed up late into the night, talking and singing freedom songs. The slow hymns and upbeat jubilant melodies drew them together in the face of danger.

Arrested by the police several times, Lewis saw the inside of many Mississippi jail cells. After each release from jail, he had a ritual.

*[I would go] to some little Dew Drop Inn . . . where I'd order a hamburger or cheese sandwich and cold soda and walk over to that jukebox and stand there with a quarter in my hand, and look over every song on that box because this choice had to be just right . . . and then I would finally drop that quarter in and punch up Marvin Gaye or Curtis Mayfield or Aretha, and I would sit down with my sandwich, and I would let that music wash over me, just wash right through me. I don't know if I've ever felt anything so sweet.*

By the end of the summer, the volunteers had registered 17,000 African American voters. Within ten years, after passage of the Voting Rights Act, the number grew to 300,000 voters. One day, Mississippi would have more elected African American officials than any other state. But those days were far off. Freedom Summer had been physically and mentally costly.

In just three months, the volunteers had endured 450 incidents of violence, including eighty beatings, thirty-five church burnings, thirty bombings, and three missing volunteers, presumed dead. Eventually, the bodies of the three volunteers were found, and someone fingered seven Klan members who allegedly had murdered them.

In addition to registering 17,000 voters that summer, volunteers had signed up 80,000 Mississippians for the MFDP. Following national procedures, MFDP members had elected their own delegates. They hoped to seat them at the Democratic National Convention. The MFDP delegates wanted to replace Mississippi's official Democratic Party delegates, who had been chosen by unfairly excluding African American voters from the selection process. Lewis and other civil rights leaders tried to get President Johnson to support their challenge.

SNCC distributed this flyer to publicize the Freedom Vote. Also pictured are voters at the polls in Miami, Florida.

Johnson, the Democratic Party's nominee, refused. He was leery of losing the support of southern Democrats. "If you seat those black buggers, the whole South will walk out," said John Connally, the governor of Texas. Connally was right. The official Mississippi delegates pledged to support Republican candidate Barry Goldwater if Johnson sat the MFDP delegates.

In August, the sixty-eight elected MFDP delegates arrived in Atlantic City, New Jersey, for the Democratic National

Convention. Many of them had traveled nearly 1,200 miles from their homes in Mississippi. Dressed in their finest clothes, they strolled down the wooden oceanfront walkway, proud and energetic, despite their long travels.

The delegates met with the convention's credentials committee to show evidence of how they had been excluded from the delegate selection process. Lewis, and millions of other Americans, watched the televised meeting. Fannie Lou Hamer, an African American activist, told of being fired, evicted, and savagely beaten by police just for registering to vote. She spoke of her struggles to get to New Jersey:

> *If the Freedom Democratic Party is not seated now, I question America. . . . Is this America, the land of the free and home of the brave, where we have to sleep with our telephones off the hooks because our lives be threatened daily because we want to live as decent human beings, in America?*

Hamer's powerful testimony moved listeners. People began to demand that the MFDP delegates be seated. President Johnson offered a compromise. The MFDP could have two seats, and a promise not to be excluded next time. The MFDP unanimously rejected the offer. Many of the official Mississippi delegates walked out of the convention, refusing to support Johnson because of his attempts at compromise. Heartbroken, many civil rights workers lost faith in the political system.

"That was a long summer, that summer of '64," Lewis recalled. "Intense. Confusing. Painful. So hopeful in the beginning, and so heartbreaking by the end."

SNCC began to unravel. Entertainer Harry Belafonte, a longtime SNCC supporter, saw the emotional and physical wounds of the sum-

Fannie Lou Hamer

mer. He was friends with Sékou Touré, the president of Guinea, a newly independent African nation. Wanting to help, Belafonte offered Lewis and eleven other activists a trip to Guinea. As the president's guests, they would tour the nation and meet with African civil rights activists. They gratefully accepted.

Lewis had long dreamed of going to Africa. The trip, his first out of the country, gave him a new perspective on black freedom movements. In Guinea, he saw blacks in charge as officials, policemen, and pilots. He realized that blacks in Africa and America faced similar struggles. Whether it was in Southwest Africa or in the southern United States, both were battling a system, held in place by white men, that controlled black people.

Lewis visited Zambia, Ethiopia, and Kenya. He took part in a week of independence celebrations in Zambia. One night, 175,000 people gathered in the new stadium. Lewis watched dancers, singers, and acrobats. A flame, like an Olympic torch, burned on a nearby hillside. Officials raised the Zambian flag. Lewis had never seen anything like this—a new nation celebrating its freedom. When he traveled to Senegal, he was toasted with glasses of banana juice and the word *uhuru*, meaning "freedom."

Later, Lewis traveled to Egypt, where he rented a camel and crossed the white desert sand. He arrived at the Great Pyramid at Giza just as the sun dipped below the horizon. Although Lewis took this stunning image home with him, he would most remember the sight of a nation celebrating its newfound independence. When he returned to the United States, however, he stepped back into the turmoil.

*Chapter* **5**

# Dark Days

S NCC was crumbling. Many civil rights workers were disillusioned. Racism wasn't just a small town or southern problem. It roots stretched wide and deep. The threats, violence, and deaths seemed endless. SNCC workers began to argue about the direction of the movement. Many of them no longer believed in nonviolent resistance. The minimal gains (in their minds) were not worth the beatings and jailings.

Americans faced violence outside of their country, too. In far-off Southeast Asia, the United States was becoming deeply involved in the divided country of Vietnam. North Vietnam was a communist country, while South Vietnam had rejected communism. In order to stop the spread of communism, the United States poured massive amounts of political, economic, and military aid into South Vietnam. After President Kennedy's assassination, President Johnson escalated U.S. involvement. Soon he was sending tens of thousands of young soldiers to Vietnam.

Lewis, as a pacifist, spoke out against the war in Vietnam, but he focused more on problems closer to home. Civil rights leaders turned their attention to Selma, Alabama. On January 18, 1965, Lewis and Martin Luther King led four hundred Selma residents to the courthouse to register. They waited in line all day, despite the freezing cold. Officials avoided registering them by hanging up a sign saying they would be out to lunch all day. The protesters' determination amazed Lewis. People walked picket lines and stood in lines at doors for hours, often knowing they would not be allowed to register that day. They waited in the rain, snow, and blazing heat. Whether facing violent deputies or standing patiently in lines, the protesters were persistent and courageous.

That evening, Lewis and King went to the Hotel Albert, Selma's finest hotel. The new Civil Rights Act made it illegal to

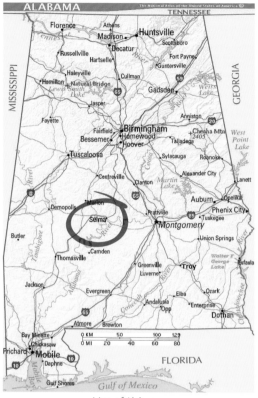

Map of Alabama

exclude African Americans, and King planned to be the hotel's first African American guest. As he signed in, a white man began punching and kicking him. Lewis grabbed the attacker, pinning his arms until the man was removed. The assault on King pushed Lewis to the edge of his commitment to nonviolence. It made him realize there were limits to a person's tolerance of not retaliating.

Each day, they led a new group of protesters to the courthouse. Soon, the federal government ordered the courthouse to open more than two days a month. Still, officials avoided registering citizens consistently. Sheriff Jim Clark, notorious for his short temper and aggression, created an armed posse to prevent blacks

King stands in front of the Hotel Albert in Selma, Alabama.

from voting by calling all adult white men to the courthouse to become deputies. More violence ensued. National media groups covered the white resistance, the mass arrests, and the brutality, especially when Clark attacked an African American woman. Each night on television, Americans watched these daily confrontations.

On February 18, 1965, an event occurred that changed everything. During a voter registration rally, Jimmie Lee Jackson, an African American army veteran, was shot. He had been trying to protect his mother from the white policeman who was beating her. Several days later, Jackson died from his wounds. Although people had endured beatings and arrests during the Selma protests, Jackson was the first to lose his life. Hundreds gathered at his funeral and listened to King's sermon.

Lewis and King planned to lead a protest march from Selma to Montgomery, fifty-four miles away. On Sunday, March 7, the marchers gathered at a church in Selma. King had received several threats on his life, so Lewis and Hosea Williams, from the SCLC, led six hundred protesters out of Selma. To leave town, they needed to cross the Edmund Pettis Bridge, an old humpbacked steel bridge adorned with a Confederate flag sign. The bridge arched high above the river, with the muddy water nearly one hundred feet below. When the marchers reached the middle of the bridge, they saw Alabama state troopers, many on horseback, waiting on the other side. Behind them stood row upon row of Alabama state troopers and Selma police. Using a bullhorn, Major John Cloud commanded the marchers to turn back, giving them two minutes to comply. Instead, the marchers knelt and began to pray.

Only one minute later, the troopers advanced. Using whips, they chased the marchers back. They viciously beat the men,

Mourners look on as Jimmie Lee Jackson's casket is carried into a church.

women, and children who fell, and trampled them with their horses. Policemen clubbed Lewis so hard, they fractured his skull. Next, they unleashed an especially toxic form of tear gas, designed to induce nausea. Lewis lay unconscious in the gray smoke. When he finally awoke, he staggered back to the church where the weeping marchers had congregated.

"I don't know how President Johnson can send troops to Vietnam . . . to the Congo . . . to Africa, and he can't send troops to Selma, Alabama," Lewis declared angrily. Reeling from his wounds, Lewis was taken to the hospital.

Coverage of the incident shocked the world. Reporters who captured the event said they had never seen such police brutality. Response to the footage was immediate. The march became known as "Bloody Sunday." Lewis recalled:

*This was a face-off in the most vivid terms between a dignified, composed, completely nonviolent multitude of silent protestors and the truly malevolent force of a heavily armed, hateful battalion of troopers. The sight of them rolling over us like human tanks was something that had never been seen before. People just couldn't believe this was happening, not in America. Women and children being attacked by armed men on horseback—it was impossible to believe.*

Pictures of Lewis being attacked appeared in the paper, too. In the hospital, he received letters and flowers from total strangers. Martin Luther King visited him and told him the march was going to happen. However, George Wallace, Alabama's governor, had forbidden the march to continue. The SCLC appealed his decision in court. While they awaited the verdict, angry citizens and civil rights activists swarmed to Selma from as far away as

Top photo: State troopers armed with billy clubs, guns, and gas masks wait for marchers to cross the Edmund Pettus Bridge. Middle photo: A state trooper rushes into a cloud of tear gas as other troopers beat protesters. Bottom photo: SNCC leader John Lewis holds his head as he is beaten by an Alabama state trooper.

New York and Minnesota. Lewis checked himself out of the hospital, against doctors' orders.

The violence mounted. Reverend James Reeb, a white minister from Boston who had come to Selma, was attacked with a baseball bat. Two days later, he died from the massive trauma to his head.

Reeb's murder was the final straw for President Johnson. On national television, he proposed a voting rights bill that would give teeth to the Fifteenth Amendment to the U.S. Constitution. Lewis, King, and other civil rights leaders gathered in the home of a friend in Selma. Squeezed together in the small living room around the television set, they watched, along with 70 million other Americans, as Johnson delivered a speech that many consider the greatest of his life. He said:

*Rarely in any time does an issue lay bare the secret heart of America itself. . . . The issue of equal rights for American Negroes is such an issue. And should we defeat every enemy, and should we double our wealth and conquer the stars and still be unequal to this issue, then we will have failed as a people and as a nation. . . . And we shall overcome.*

Soon after, a judge ruled that the march to Montgomery could continue. The number of marchers grew to 25,000. Some of them would march fifty-four miles in five days. President Johnson ordered nearly 4,000 armed guards and snipers to line the entire route. Helicopters and planes would patrol from the air.

Lewis and other leaders began to organize the giant march. They printed and distributed maps and schedules. They ordered carnival-sized tents where the marchers would sleep. They gathered pots, pans, and stoves for cooking. Women made sand-

Reverend King carries a wreath as he and others make their way toward a memorial service for Unitarian minister Reverend James Reeb. From left to right (front): His Eminence Iakobos, archbishop of the Greek Orthodox Church, King, Reverends Ralph Abernathy and Andrew Young.

wiches around the clock. Doctors readied hundreds of boxes of bandages to ease blistered feet.

On March 1, the protesters left Selma and headed down Highway 80 into the Alabama countryside. They passed swampy marshes, red clay farmland, and thin winding streams. The crowd included people from all over the country, of all ages, races, and religions. On the first day, the marchers walked seven miles. That night they ate, built campfires, and sang songs before bedding down in the tents. Although Lewis would walk the entire route, each night he returned by car to Selma. Doctors feared that sleeping on the cold, hard ground would worsen his head injury.

They walked through the sun, rain, and wind for the next three days. On the last night, the weary marchers stopped to celebrate outside of Montgomery. Nearly 20,000 people gathered under the stars, singing songs and listening to speeches.

The next day, the crowd grew to 50,000. They marched into Montgomery, past the fountain in the city's square where slaves had watered their owners' horses. A Confederate flag flew high from the courthouse. The crowd walked to the steps of the state's silver and white capitol building. Governor Wallace watched from his office, behind drawn blinds, as the triumphant crowd listened to speeches. They held up a petition requesting the governor to remove the obstacles to voter registration.

Four and half months later, on August 6, Congress passed President Johnson's proposed Voting Rights Bill. The law ended literacy tests and poll taxes. It also called for the appointment of federal officials to register voters in southern counties where discrimination had occurred. Within two years, approximately 430,000 black voters registered across the South. Change came quickly. Soon voters elected Julian Bond, an African American worker from SNCC, to the Georgia legislature.

President Johnson had invited Lewis to attend the ceremonial signing of the bill. Afterward, he gave Lewis a pen he used to sign the document. Lewis framed the pen, along with a copy of the bill. He would remember the Selma march as one of the country's finest hours. "There was never a march like this one before and there hasn't been one since," Lewis said. "You saw the power of the most powerful country on the face of the earth."

Marchers carrying banner lead way as 15,000 parade in Harlem.

Selma was one of the last nonviolent acts of the civil rights movement. Many activists continued to become more militant. Changes within SNCC threatened Lewis's position as chairman. Stokely Carmichael pushed for SNCC to be an all-black organization. Although Lewis believed the movement should be led by African Americans, he also believed in the Beloved Community. He wanted SNCC to represent that community, with people of different races working together to end discrimination. To Lewis's dismay, many white staffers were asked to leave.

SNCC workers elected Carmichael as their new chairman. Although deeply saddened by the turn SNCC was taking, Lewis stayed on as a worker. In June 1966, he and Carmichael attended a rally in Mississippi. Carmichael urged listeners to strike back at white power. When Lewis gave a speech urging nonviolence, the audience walked out. A month later, Lewis cleaned out his desk and left SNCC for good. At twenty-six years old, Lewis was starting his life over again. He had no money, no job, no family, and no home.

Lewis took a job with the Field Foundation, a charity in New York City. "As I rode the train up from Atlanta, I felt more lonesome than I had ever felt in my life," he wrote. "I had lived a lifetime in the past six years, and now the rest of my life lay ahead of me, without a map, without a blueprint."

In New York, Lewis found a small apartment, where he survived on toast and chicken pot pies. He missed the life he had known. He sadly watched the SNCC he had known wither, as militants like Julius Lester filled key positions. Lester advocated for vengeance, and urged African Americans to hate the white community.

In New York, Lewis had many new experiences. He traveled with friends and explored the grassy dunes and steep cliffs of beaches in New England. Despite finding new friendships, the size of New York City overwhelmed him. He missed the small, close-knit communities he had known in the South.

After one year, Lewis moved back to Atlanta. There were many more battles to fight in the South. Although illegal, job discrimination was rampant. Most of Lewis's brothers, like many other

Stokely Carmichael, age twenty-five, became the head of SNCC in 1966. He introduced the phrase "Black Power" to the civil rights movement.

African Americans in the South, had moved north in hopes of finding better work. One brother remained in the South, living in a rented shack and working as a woodcutter.

Lewis took a job as a community organizer with the Southern Regional Council. He traveled across the South, helping to strengthen communities by organizing co-ops. Although African Americans could now vote and had other rights, many struggled with basic needs—shelter, food, and jobs.

During this time, Lewis also spoke out against the continuing Vietnam War. Thousands of U.S. soldiers in Vietnam were dying at alarming rates. Many Americans opposed the country's involvement. They questioned the objectives of the war and resisted the draft. Nearly 35,000 men were being drafted each month, many of them black. Although 10 percent of the population in America was black, 25 percent of the fatalities in Vietnam were black soldiers. U.S. troops were fighting for the rights of people in South Vietnam, but, "the black American soldier has himself never experienced democracy," said Reverend King.

As Lewis denounced the war, he continued his job as a community organizer. He also earned his degree at Fisk University, taking the final courses he was missing. He worked and studied hard, but found time for friends, too.

In 1967, Lewis went with friends to a small New Year's Eve party in Atlanta. They introduced him to Lillian Miles. Intelligent and attractive, Lillian had spent time in Africa as a Peace Corps volunteer. She worked as a librarian at Atlanta University. Lewis found her easy to talk to, and especially liked when she defended Martin Luther King during an argument at the party.

Lewis wanted to see Lillian again. He decided to throw himself a birthday party and invite her. He bought a new record player and cooked a big batch of barbeque wings, his specialty. Lillian showed up wearing a dress covered with peace symbols. She was drawn to Lewis, too. Although he was a key leader in the civil rights movement, he was shy and humble. The two began to date regularly. On weekends they went out to dinner, watched movies, and spent evenings playing Scrabble.

Other aspects of Lewis's life improved, as well. Until then, he had little contact with his family. His arrests and involvement in the civil rights movement had shamed them. Now he began to reconcile those relationships. Life was quiet for the moment.

In 1968, a presidential election year, President Johnson announced that he would not be running against the Republican contender, Richard Milhous Nixon. Johnson had grown increasingly unpopular because of his policies in Vietnam. President Kennedy's younger brother, Robert, announced his intentions to run for president. He strongly opposed Johnson's actions in Vietnam and was deeply committed to civil rights and helping the poor.

Lewis sent Kennedy a telegram offering his support. Two days later, Kennedy asked Lewis to help with the campaign. Lewis took a leave of absence from his position as a community organizer and flew to Indianapolis to begin working. His goal was to register more African American voters and encourage them to support Kennedy in the upcoming Indiana primary.

On April 4, 1968, as Lewis waited in Indianapolis for Kennedy to arrive at a rally, he heard tragic news. Late that afternoon, Martin Luther King had been assassinated by James Earl Ray, a white racist. Ray had shot King when he stepped out onto the balcony of the Lorraine Hotel, where he was staying in Memphis. The news stunned Lewis and numbed him. He stood motionless in the cold wind, unable to move or think.

Unlike today where news travels instantly, reports of King's assassination had not widely spread when Kennedy arrived. Together, he and Lewis agreed that Kennedy would break the news at the rally. Kennedy spoke honesty to the predominantly African American crowd. He appealed to them not as blacks or whites, but as human beings. He said:

*. . . . But the vast majority of white people and the vast majority of black people in this country want to live together, want to improve the quality of our life, and want justice for all human beings who abide in our land. Let us dedicate ourselves to what the Greeks wrote so many years ago: to tame the savageness of man and to make gentle the life of this world.*

Although Indianapolis remained quiet that night, King's assassination sparked riots in more than seventy towns and cities. Despite the efforts of more than 70,000 federal troops, the night left forty-six people dead. People were fueled by the words of men such as Stokely Carmichael. He said King's assassination was a declaration of war. Carmichael urged African Americans to arm themselves with weapons for the battle against white people.

Lewis flew back to Atlanta and helped to prepare for King's funeral. Thousands paraded past his casket in Atlanta. The church couldn't hold everyone who wanted to hear his service. Nearly 100,000 people listened outside on loudspeakers. Many of them marched afterward in the funeral procession that carried King to the cemetery. In the hot, humid spring weather, Lillian stood by Lewis's side at King's grave. When Lewis went home, he grieved alone. "Dr. King was my friend, my brother, my leader," Lewis stated. King "made me who I am. When he was killed, I really felt I'd lost a part of myself."

To Lewis, Robert Kennedy still represented hope for the civil rights movement. He threw himself back into the campaign, and

Robert F. Kennedy

traveled to Oregon and California. Lewis put up signs, talked to people, gave speeches, and canvassed voters door-to-door. Polls showed that Kennedy was gaining ground.

On June 4, Lewis joined campaign staffers at a hotel in Los Angeles to watch the primary returns. Results soon showed that Kennedy had won the California primary. Downstairs in the hotel's ballroom, Kennedy gave a triumphant speech. As he headed upstairs to join the celebration, a waiting assassin, Sirhan Sirhan, shot him. Lewis heard the screams and saw the news on television. He fell to his knees, sobbing. He wandered the streets until early in the morning. Within hours, Kennedy passed away.

On Lewis's flight back home the next morning, he wept the entire way. King's assassination had been only two months earlier. "We lost something with the deaths of those two leaders that year . . . that as a nation we will never recover," he stated. "Call it innocence or trust."

Lewis attended Kennedy's funeral at St. Patrick's Cathedral in New York. Later, the mourners traveled by train, winding their way to Arlington National Cemetery in Washington, D.C., for Kennedy's burial. "The sense of hope, of optimism, of possibility, was replaced by horror, the worst of times, the feeling that maybe, just maybe, we would not overcome," Lewis wrote. "It was a dark, dark time."

Although still distraught, Lewis traveled to the Democratic National Convention in Chicago. He and other Democrats from Georgia challenged Georgia's official delegates, claiming their selection was biased, like Mississippi's. In a compromise, the two delegations split the votes. Later that year, Republican Richard Nixon was elected president. Nixon would eventually end the Vietnam War, but not until an estimated 58,226 American soldiers had been killed, along with at least 5 million Vietnamese soldiers and civilians.

After the convention, Lewis returned to Atlanta. Emotionally and physically exhausted, he collapsed. Doctors checked him into a hospital for rest. Lillian canceled her plans for a vacation and spent time with him in the hospital. She visited each morning, bringing him the daily paper and his mail. While lying in his hospital bed, he proposed to her, and she accepted.

The couple married in 1968, four days before Christmas. Martin Luther King Sr. performed the ceremony. Three hundred family members and friends helped celebrate. Amid the troubling time for the country, Lewis's new life held promise and hope.

Chapter

6

A New Path

Soon after Lewis and Lillian married, they bought a home in Atlanta on a shady, tree-lined street. The Lewises were the first black family in the neighborhood. Some of their neighbors made them feel unwelcome, as they wanted the area to stay segregated. Integration was occurring in small towns and in big cities across the country, but many people had difficulty learning to live together.

Change came slowly, especially in the South. Although the Voting Rights Act had reformed many aspects of voting, African Americans in some areas still feared registering to vote. Threats and violence often deterred them from casting their ballots.

The Southern Regional Council had created a Voter Education Project (VEP), and they hired Lewis as the head of the program. He organized voter registration drives, led citizenship education classes, and arranged transportation to courthouses and polling places.

Lewis also monitored state laws that affected voting. In 1971, several counties in Mississippi erased all existing voter registration, forcing everyone to re-register. Lewis, Julian Bond, Fannie Lou Hamer, and Coretta Scott King barnstormed the state to re-register African American voters.

On August 6, 1976, John and Lillian adopted a baby boy, whom they named John Miles. It was a happy time in their lives.

A few months later, Lewis attended a reunion for SNCC workers. No longer bitter about the path SNCC's leaders had chosen, he enjoyed seeing old friends and co-workers. They talked about the changes in their lives. When the conversation turned to politics, several people asked Lewis if he was ever going to run for political office. It was something Lewis had been considering over the previous several years. Soon after the reunion, he got his chance.

Four years earlier, voters in Georgia had elected Andrew Young, an African American, to Congress. They reelected him again in 1974 and 1976. Early in his third term, he resigned to work for America's new president, Jimmy Carter, as an ambassador to the United Nations. He left his congressional seat empty.

Lewis weighed many factors. He had political, financial, and personal concerns about running for office. Although as an activist Lewis had worked with politicians, he had no true background in politics. Despite his years of giving speeches, he was not a charismatic speaker. To wage his political campaign, he would need to give up his VEP position; if he lost, he would be unemployed. Campaigning would not only eat into his finances, but also into his time with Lillian and John Miles.

The biggest factor in his decision, though, was his desire to make America a stronger, fairer country. Lewis had often risked his life for this noble cause. Despite all the reasons not to run, Lillian encouraged him. She also had an interest in politics. Active and outgoing, she wanted to see change. As a politician in Washington, D.C., Lewis would have the ability to improve people's lives. Together, he and Lillian decided to launch his first political campaign.

The election to fill Young's congressional seat was a fusion election. Twelve candidates, Democrats and Republicans, would compete in one race. Young had represented Georgia's Fifth Congressional District. The makeup of the district was 57 percent white and 43 percent black. Lewis, wanting to represent all of the citizens in the district, regardless of race, said he wouldn't campaign solely for African American votes.

During the campaign, Lewis met with voters and listened to their concerns. Although his speeches were unpolished, they were sincere. Martin Luther King Sr., Coretta Scott King, and Andrew Young gave Lewis their support. The *Atlanta Constitution* endorsed him, too.

On March 15, 1977, voters went to the polls. When the results came in, no candidate had won more than 50 percent of the vote. Officials would hold a run-off election between the top two candidates—Lewis and Wyche Fowler, the city council's president.

Lewis and Fowler, who was white, were alike in many ways. The same age, they both held broad appeal with black and white voters. They also had liberal stances and nearly identical stands on issues. Fowler, however, had more political experience on his side.

Lewis campaigned vigorously. However, on April 4, voters elected Fowler in a landslide. He won 62 percent of the vote to Lewis's 38 percent. Although Lewis had lost, and racked up $50,000 in debt from campaign costs, he had enjoyed campaigning. The experience cemented his decision to one day become a congressman.

Later that year, Lewis's family suffered a different kind of loss. Eddie Lewis, John's father, passed away. He had suffered a stroke a year earlier, and never fully recovered. Lewis's mother was devastated. They had raised ten children and faced great adversity together. Lewis returned home and delivered the eulogy at the funeral service. Lewis's father had been well liked and respected in their small community, and many people attended his funeral. He was buried at the small church near their home. Although John Lewis's civil rights work had once severed his ties with his family, time had healed those wounds.

When Lewis returned to work after his father's funeral, he received a great honor. President Jimmy Carter offered him a position as the associate director of ACTION, a federal agency

that ran social programs. The organization made use of volunteers, both
young and old, to better the country. They ran VISTA, a domestic
peace corps program; RSVP, a program that utilized retired seniors as
volunteers; and FGP, a foster grandparents program. Lewis would direct
125 staffers and oversee 235,000 volunteers. In 1977, he and Lillian moved
to Washington, D.C., to a home near
ACTION's headquarters. From Lewis's
corner office, he could see the White House.

Top photo: John Lewis poses for a 1969 family
picture. His parents are seated in the front
row, and Lewis is standing, the second
from the left. Jimmy Carter on the right.

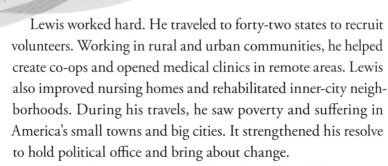

Lewis worked hard. He traveled to forty-two states to recruit volunteers. Working in rural and urban communities, he helped create co-ops and opened medical clinics in remote areas. Lewis also improved nursing homes and rehabilitated inner-city neighborhoods. During his travels, he saw poverty and suffering in America's small towns and big cities. It strengthened his resolve to hold political office and bring about change.

In November 1981, Lewis took another political chance. He ran for the Atlanta City Council. He campaigned across the city from dawn until dusk. Often he distributed leaflets at night outside of all-night grocery stores. Determined to win, he attended meetings and dinners and gave speeches. Lewis won the seat with 70 percent of the vote.

Over his first four years in office, Lewis became a strong representative, valued for his honesty and fairness. When he served on the Public Safety Committee, he befriended nearly every police officer and fire fighter. In 1985, Atlanta voters reelected him for another term. He won 85 percent of the vote. However, Lewis made enemies when he criticized some of his fellow council members for their conflicts of interest. When one member sponsored a highway project that would profit his trucking company by $1 million, Lewis ordered income disclosures for all council members. As a result, he alienated himself and often was unable to get his proposed bills passed.

In 1986, Lewis got another chance at a congressional seat when Wyche Fowler ran for Senate and left his seat vacant. It had been nine years since Lewis's loss to Fowler. In that time, Lewis had become politically wiser, learning more about government through his work as a councilman.

Lewis announced his candidacy in February. Although he would run against a field of nine candidates, his main opponent was Julian Bond. A Georgia state senator, Bond was also Lewis's friend and former SNCC colleague. He was the best known of all the candidates, and the favorite of Democrats and African Americans in Atlanta. He had the most experience, and he quickly staked an early lead in the polls. The Democratic leaders who had supported Lewis in 1977 now endorsed Bond.

Despite their friendship, Lewis was out to win. He was competitive and determined, and he ran a tough campaign. Each morning, he rose before dawn to meet voters on their way to work. Late into the night, he was still talking with voters outside of theaters and all-night grocery stores. Lewis wore out three pairs of running shoes jogging door-to-door to meet voters. He listened to them and shared the story of his life, from being the son of sharecroppers to preaching to chickens. He even developed trigger thumb, a condition well known to many politicians. The ligaments at the base of his thumb became strained and swollen from shaking so many hands. Sometimes his thumb cramped down against his palm. In the early morning it was especially painful, as he pulled his thumb back into place.

Bond remained his toughest opponent. Although he and Lewis had both been civil rights activists, the similarities ended there. They looked, sounded, and acted differently. Tall and well spoken, Bond was once ranked as one of America's most handsome men, and described as a "cool poet and wordsmith." Short and less articulate, Lewis was described as "balding, dark, scowling"; "built like a bulldog"; and "as real as a pine knot."

The two men's characters were dissimilar, as well. It was tough for Lewis to point out those differences, but he did. The election was not about their friendship. Lewis jabbed at Bond's record as a senator, stating that he had missed several votes on bills. He also poked at Bond's popularity with the media. Bond had recently hosted the late-night television show *Saturday Night Live.* Some people argued that Bond's media coverage interfered with his job as a politician. Lewis also pointed out that although Bond had brought in more money in endorsements, the majority of it came from outside of the district he was campaigning to represent in Congress.

Lewis's doggedness paid off. The day before the election, the *Atlanta Journal-Constitution* endorsed him. The paper stated:

> *John Lewis is not the snappiest talker in this amazingly articulate field. He may not always be the first on the scene of a trendy new issue, but he is a thoughtful, dedicated, dead-honest man who steadily works himself toward positions that are both reasonable and, precisely because he has thought them out with care, usually durable.*

In August 1986, voters went to the polls. Bond won most of the votes, but fell short of the majority. He and Lewis had received the most votes of the nine candidates. The two men would face each other in a run-off election. They each had three more weeks to campaign.

When Bond challenged Lewis to a series of five debates, people said it would clinch Bond's election. They predicted Lewis would compare unfavorably on television, because of his appearance and speaking style. However, Lewis had been polishing his speaking skills with public speaking lessons. He also was working with media consultant Shawn Reed. She taught Lewis how to deal with the press effectively. She coached him on his appearance, such as which clothes to wear. To prepare him for the debate, she grilled him with questions. Lewis needed to show voters how he differed from Bond. Reed told Lewis that instead of cramming answers and becoming nervous before the debate,

he should relax in a hot tub. Lewis listened. An hour later, he
toweled off and headed downtown for the debate.

Lewis's thorough preparation caught Bond off guard. There
were no surprises for Lewis, though. He handled himself well,
speaking clearly and effectively. Afterward, Bond's lead slipped.
Soon the gap narrowed further.

On September 2, 1986, voters cast their ballots. At first, exit
polls showed Bond leading. Then the results tightened. By 2:00
a.m., Lewis had staged an amazing upset, winning the election by a 4 percent margin. An hour later, he and his entourage
walked from their headquarters to their downtown hotel ballroom to celebrate. At first they numbered forty. By the time they
reached the hotel, little more than a mile away, their triumphant
group had swelled to four hundred people. "I thought to myself
that with all the walking I had done in my life, with all the
marches I had ever made, this was the sweetest," Lewis recalled.

Later that month in the general election, Lewis defeated the Republican candidate Portia Scott by a landslide. He and his supporters hired a special railroad car to take them to Washington, D.C., for his swearing-in ceremony in January. They dubbed the car the "Freedom Train."

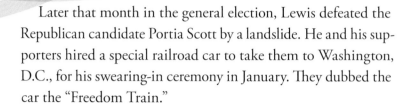

John Lewis, left, and his wife, Lillian, holding hands, lead supporters on a march from his campaign headquarters to an Atlanta hotel for a victory party after he defeated Julian Bond on September 3, 1986.

*Chapter*

# 7

# The Beloved Community

In January 1987, John Lewis was sworn in as a member of the 100th Congress. He stood out among his colleagues. As one of the top civil rights leaders in the country, Lewis had helped change the history of the United States. Many fellow congressmen made special efforts to meet him. "I've seen courage in action on many occasions," said Senator John McCain. "I can't say I've seen anyone possess more of it, or use it for any better purpose and to any greater effect, than John Lewis."

Lewis threw himself into his work. He attended every meeting and accepted every invitation to speak. His quickly learned the workings of the House and his role as a congressman. During Lewis's first term, he served on several committees. Soon he was credited with improving highways, public transportation, and federal offices. During Lewis's first year in office, he was one of only twelve House members with a perfect voting record. He didn't miss a single vote on a bill.

Lewis kept up a grueling work schedule, rising early each morning. He lived in a home in Washington that was much different than his childhood home. He worked in his Capitol office building, instead of the cotton fields he once picked. Working

A view of downtown Atlanta at dusk

long hours each day, he met with his committees, gave interviews, and attended to his duties in the House. Every Friday, he met with his constituents, seeing anyone who had an issue to discuss. On weekends, Lewis flew home to Atlanta to attend community functions and spend time with his family.

Lillian and John Miles still lived at their home in Atlanta. Although at first the family had planned to move to Washington together, they decided that staying in Atlanta would be best. Lillian could continue her work as a librarian; she would become a top administrator at Clark-Atlanta University. John Miles wouldn't have to switch schools or move away from his close friends. During the summer, they joined Lewis in Washington.

Lewis easily won reelection to a second term. Throughout his years in office, he continued to fight for the causes he had long supported. For example, he remained dedicated to pacifism and nonviolence. Early in 1991, he was one of a handful of congressmen to oppose the Gulf War in the Middle East. In August 1990, Iraq had invaded the neighboring country of Kuwait. President George H. W. Bush sent U.S troops into Kuwait to oust Iraq. Although the Iraqis were quickly thwarted, Lewis disagreed with

the president's methods. People noted Lewis's independence and willingness to speak his mind.

In 1991, Speaker of the House of Representatives Thomas Foley nominated Lewis for a key leadership position. Lewis became one of the three deputy Democratic whips. Each party's whip counts votes and persuades members to support certain legislation. He soon was elected the chief whip, becoming the highest-ranking elected African American official in the United States.

Lewis remained true to his ideal of the Beloved Community. He supported people because of their views and positions on issues, not because of the color of their skin. When President George H. W. Bush nominated Clarence Thomas, an African American, as a Supreme Court justice, Lewis carefully considered Thomas's views. A conservative, Thomas disagreed with Lewis on many issues. Although Lewis eventually voted against Thomas's confirmation, he carefully considered the appointment and met with Thomas to discuss his views.

Lewis remained fair and open-minded. When he met candidates he liked, he didn't hesitate to support them. He and two other African American congressmen backed Arkansas governor Bill Clinton in his bid for the presidency. Lewis pledged "friendship and support to me when only my mother and my wife thought I could be elected," said Clinton after he was elected president in 1992.

That same year, Atlanta voters reelected Lewis with 75 percent of the vote. He also gained a seat on the House Ways and Means Committee. The influential committee controls all of the money appropriated by the House. The oldest and most prestigious committee in Congress, its members are responsible for taxes, Social Security, Medicare, unemployment benefits, foster care, adoption programs, and child support laws.

For the first two years of Clinton's presidency, the Democratic Party held the majority in the House. In 1994, however, Republicans gained the majority for the first time in forty years. Much of the Republican Party's strategy was planned by Newt Gingrich, who became the new speaker of the House.

Lewis and Gingrich's districts adjoined, and the two men often were at odds with each other. Lewis criticized many of the bills that Gingrich sponsored. Gingrich proposed loosening restrictions on the Clean Water Act, scaling back school lunch programs, and ending the "motor voter" law that allowed voters to register when they renewed their driver's license.

Lewis's most explosive confrontation with Gingrich arose over proposed cuts to Medicare, the federal program that provides health benefits to the elderly. Both Lewis and Gingrich were invited to speak at a Medicare conference in Atlanta. Lewis grabbed headlines by leading a demonstration of protesters outside of the conference to bring attention to the funding cuts. Gingrich refused to speak in the presence of the protesters. He suggested to reporters that Lewis should decide if he was a congressman or a demonstrator. Lewis retorted that protests were necessary to dramatize, educate, and sensitize people to issues. Members of Congress still have the right to protest, he said. "Dr. King used to say, 'The time is

Newt Gingrich

always right to protest for what is right,'" Lewis said. "I believe in that."

Soon Lewis protested again. In October 1995, influential African American leader Louis Farrakhan—leader of the Nation of Islam—led the Million Man March to Washington, D.C. Approximately one million black men gathered to demonstrate their commitment to their families and the black communities, and to counteract the image of black men portrayed in the media. Although Lewis had risked his life to promote equality for African Americans, he stated publicly that he would not attend. Lewis had several reasons for his decision. Farrakhan was a controversial figure, who had made negative remarks about Jewish and homosexual people. Although Farrakhan intended to bring positive attention to the African American community, Lewis disliked that the march excluded black women, as well as people of different races. He called it an effort to resegregate America. Lewis still strived for a truly interracial democracy in which people of all races worked together to solve problems.

In 1998, Lewis published an autobiography entitled *Walking with the Wind*. During the writing process, he revisited sites from his past and recorded his memories. The book received rave reviews. It won several awards, such as the Robert F. Kennedy Book Award, and was named the *New York Times* Notable Book of the Year. The library in Troy, Alabama, where Lewis had grown up, invited him to speak. They presented him with a library card, more than forty years after they had refused him one.

The area where Lewis had grown up had changed greatly. Pike County Training School, once the only option for African American students, no longer existed. The nearby town of Brundidge, Alabama, held a John Lewis Day and named a street after him. That same weekend, Troy State University—formerly

An aerial view of the Million Man March on Washington, D.C.

Troy State College, which had ignored Lewis's application admission—held a luncheon in his honor. Their segregated views had led to Lewis's meeting with Martin Luther King, and set him along his path in activism.

By the year 2000, Lewis had been elected to seven terms in Congress. When Paul Coverdell, a U.S. senator from Georgia, died suddenly in office, people talked about appointing Lewis to serve out Coverdell's unfinished term. Lewis had considered becoming a senator by running against Coverdell in 1997. However, he decided to continue representing his district instead.

The following year, on September 11, 2001, coordinated terrorist attacks in New York City and Washington, D.C., stunned Lewis and the world. Terrorists hijacked four planes, crashing two into the Twin Towers of the World Trade Center in New York, another into the Pentagon in Washington, D.C, and the fourth into a field in Pennsylvania. Some 3,000 people died in the attacks. Lewis pointed out that terrorists can destroy buildings, but they cannot break the spirit of freedom and the love of democracy. Lewis had put his body on the line for many years, carrying that spirit inside him.

In later years, Lewis opposed many of President George W. Bush's policies, including the country's involvement in a war against terror that led to the U.S. invasion of Iraq. President Bush had little international support for the war, and many argued that the war had unclear objectives. The war has continued for many years, in the face of much American opposition.

As of 2009, Lewis had represented Georgia for twenty-three years. No other Georgia senator or congressman has served longer. He still keeps up his demanding work schedule. He has played a role in passing legislation addressing needs in education, health, the environment, crime, and much more. He continues to use his position in the House to make the nation fairer for people of all races, ages, and religions. At times, that has meant supporting an increase in the minimum wage, providing more funding for community outreach programs, and improving care for senior citizens. He is a member of more than forty caucuses that meet to define policy on topics ranging from adoption to cystic fibrosis to foreign wars to preserving historical sites.

Lewis has received many honors for his work during the civil rights movement and as a congressman. He holds more than fifty honorary degrees from prestigious colleges and universities. He has been awarded the Lincoln Medal from Ford's Theater, the Martin Luther King Jr. Nonviolent Peace Prize, the John F. Kennedy Profile in Courage Award, and numerous others. A John Lewis Award honors people who have made outstanding contributions to society. The John Lewis Scholarship Fund provides financial aid to students who show a commitment to protecting human rights through nonviolent means.

Nearly fifty years after the Freedom Ride, many of the participants, including Lewis and Jim Zwerg, met and shared memories of those violent and terrifying rides. Every year, Lewis leads a reenactment of the Selma marches. Crowds gather to walk across the Edmund Pettis Bridge.

Lewis hunts for special artifacts related to the civil rights movement. He often peruses flea markets for rare books about African Americans. His greatest find was in a cobwebbed shop in Alexandria, Virginia, where he discovered a copy of Martin Luther King's book *Stride Toward Freedom*. Tucked inside the book was a program from a church service in 1960 featuring a sermon by King. He had autographed the book, wishing its owner well. Lewis paid fifty cents for the book. It remains his treasure, as he has nothing else signed by his idol. The cher-

ished book is a tangible reminder of some of the finest, proudest moments of his life.

Lewis, and countless others, fought to bring great change to the United States. Because of their sacrifices, African Americans are no longer prevented from exercising their guaranteed rights. In an amazing turn of events since this country's onset, Americans in November 2008 elected an African American man, Barack Obama, as their president.

Although Lewis originally supported a different candidate, Hillary Clinton, he switched his support when he saw a movement of hope amassing behind Obama. He said:

*People have been afraid to hope again, to believe again. We have lost great leaders: John F. Kennedy, Martin, Robert Kennedy. And so people might have questioned whether or not to place their full faith in a symbol and a leader. The danger of disappointment is immense, the problems are so big. None of them can be solved in a day or a year. And that's the way it was with the civil rights movement. This is the struggle of a lifetime. We play our part and fulfill our role.*

For Lewis, Obama's inauguration was filled with emotion. Just one day after the nation celebrated Martin Luther King Jr. Day, Lewis watched as Obama was sworn in as the country's new president. In 1950, few would have believed such an achievement would be possible.

Lewis is the only remaining speaker alive from the March on Washington, in which Martin Luther King told Americans about his dream. From the same view atop the Lincoln Memorial, Lewis had looked out across the Mall and seen thousands of people who wanted change. At Obama's inauguration, forty-

President Barack Obama and John Lewis

six years later, Lewis again looked out at a sea of people young and old, from far and near, of all races, who came to witness a change in American history.

Without the work of John Lewis, and so many other brave people during the civil rights movement, the Voting Rights Act might not have been passed. An African American man might not have been elected president. "Barack Obama is what comes at the end of that bridge in Selma," Lewis said.

Still, despite having come so far, Lewis says there are many strides to make toward the Beloved Community. His work toward that goal has changed people's lives, even those who once fiercely opposed equal rights for African Americans.

In February 2009, days after Obama's inauguration, one of the men who beat Lewis in the Rock Hill, South Carolina, bus station during the Freedom Ride came forward. Elwin Wilson, who had once hung a black doll from a noose outside his home, traveled to Washington and met with Lewis in his Capitol Hill office. He humbly offered an apology, forty-eight years after his attack.

Despite the many changes, Americans still face difficulties. Racism continues, and in recent years the country has been troubled by terrorism, environmental problems, and a worsening economy. When Lewis worries that America is bursting at its seams, he recalls a story from his youth.

As a young boy, Lewis was spending the afternoon playing with his cousins at his Uncle Rabbit's house up the road. As a storm approached, the sky turned black. Howling winds swirled the dirt in the front yard, and lightning split the sky. The children herded into the small house, which began to shake. The plank floor buckled and a corner of the house lifted up. The children clasped hands, lined up, and walked to the corner, keeping the house on the ground. They walked back and forth as the wind screamed and the rain beat the tin roof.

John Lewis is pictured here with Elwin Wilson of Rock Hill, South Carolina, in Lewis's Washington, D.C., office February 3, 2009, while taping an interview for *Good Morning America*. Wilson, part of a white gang in 1961 that jeered Lewis, attacked him, and left Lewis bloodied on the ground in South Carolina, met with the congressman so he could apologize and express regret for his hatred.

Together, with the weight of their small bodies, they kept the house down until the storm blew over. Lewis wrote that his life and American society remind him of that day:

> *Children holding hands, walking with the wind. That is America to me—not just the movement for civil rights, but the endless struggle to respond with decency, dignity, and a sense of brotherhood to all the challenges that face us as a nation, as a whole. That is the story, in essence, of my life, of the path to which I've been committed since I turned from a boy to a man, and to which I remain committed today.*

# Timeline

**1940**
Born on February 21 in Dunn's Chapel, Alabama.

**1953**
Begins attending Pike County Training School.

**1957**
Attends American Baptist Theological Seminary in Nashville, Tennessee.

**1958**
Begins to study nonviolent resistance; meets Martin Luther King, Jr.

**1959**
Cofounds the Nashville Student Movement.

**1960**
Organizes lunch counter sit-ins in Nashville.

**1961**
Joins the Student Nonviolent Coordinating Committee (SNCC); graduates from American Baptist Theological Seminary; becomes a Freedom Rider.

**1962**
Attends Fisk University.

**1963**
Elected chairman of SNCC; gives a speech on August 28 at the March on Washington; moves to Atlanta.

**1964**
Helps lead the Freedom Summer voter registration project in Mississippi.

**1965**
Leads the "Bloody Sunday" march for voting rights on March 7; leads the Selma march for voter registration from March 21 to 25.

**1966**
Begins to work for the Field Foundation; ousted as SNCC chairman.

**1967**
Graduates from Fisk University; works as a community organizer for the Southern Regional Council.

**1968**
Campaigns for Robert F. Kennedy's presidential campaign; marries Lillian Miles.

**1970**
Becomes the director of the Southern Regional Council's Voter Education Project (VEP).

**1976**
Becomes a father, when he and Lillian adopt their son John Miles.

**1977**
Appointed head of ACTION; makes an unsuccessful run for the U.S. House of Representatives.

**1981**
Elected to the Atlanta City Council.

**1986**
Elected to Congress as a U.S. representative of Georgia (has been reelected every two years since).

**1996**
Appointed chief deputy whip of the U.S. House, becoming the highest-ranking African American elected official in the U.S.

**1998**
Publishes *Walking with the Wind: A Memoir of the Movement*.

**2001**
Receives the John F. Kennedy Profile in Courage Award for Lifetime Achievement.

**2008**
Endorses African American U.S. Senator Barack Obama for president.

**2009**
Watches Barack Obama's inauguration atop the Lincoln Memorial.

# Sources

## Chapter One: A Sharecropper's Son

p. 12,   "moral leader who…" "Biography of John Lewis," *U.S. Congressman John Lewis,* http://johnlewis.house.gov/index. php?option=com_content&task=view&id=17&Itemid=31.

p. 12,   "Because of you…" David Remnick, "The President's Hero," *New Yorker,* February 2, 2009.

p. 18,   "It was a small…" John Lewis, *Walking with the Wind* (New York: Simon & Schuster, 1998), 30.

p. 19,   "This was true…" Ibid., 46.

p. 20,   "I fell in love…" Christine Hill, *John Lewis: From Freedom Rider to Congressman* (Berkeley Heights, NJ: Enslow Publishers, 2002), 15.

p. 25,   "took the words…" Ibid., 18.

p. 27,   "Thinking about…" Ibid., 19.

## Chapter Two: Taking a Stand

p. 37,   "All my life…" Lewis, *Walking with the Wind,* 94.

p. 39,   "It was really…" Hill, *John Lewis,* 28.

p. 40,   "I had never…" Lewis, *Walking with the Wind,* 115.

p. 41,   "Growing up in…" Hill, *John Lewis,* 29.

p. 42,   "I lost my…" Ann Bausum, *Freedom Riders: John Lewis and Jim Zwerg on  the Front Lines of the Civil Rights Movement* (Washington: National Geographic, 2006), 32.

p. 42,   "At this time…" Lewis, *Walking with the Wind,* 133.

## Chapter Three: Freedom Rider

p. 47,   "You will never…" "Freedom Rides," *The Martin Luther King Research and Education Institute,* http://www.m1kkpp01. stanford.edu/index.php/kingpapers/aricle/freedom_rides.

p. 49,   "Every decent…" Bausum, *Freedom Riders,* 40.

p. 49,   "If not us…" Ibid., 6.

p. 53,   "We were forced…" Hill, *John Lewis,* 42.

p. 54,   "We used to…" Ibid., 42.

p. 54,   "There was…" Bausum, *Freedom Riders,* 7.

p. 56,   "[They] never understood why…" Hill, *John Lewis,* 43.

## Chapter Four: Freedom Summer

p. 58,    "In the name…" Wyn Craig Wade, *The Ku Klux Klan in America: The Fiery Cross* (New York: Oxford University Press, 1987), 321.

p. 61,    "We are confronted…" "Pre 1965: Events Leading to the Creating of EEOC," *The U.S. Equal Employment Opportunity Commission*, http://www.eeoc.gov/about/eeoc/35th/pre1965/index.html.

p. 63,    "By the force…" Hill, *John Lewis,* 49.

p. 63,    "I have a dream…" Kerry A. Graves, *I Have a Dream: The Story Behind Martin Luther King Jr.'s Most Famous Speech* (Philadelphia, PA: Chelsea House Publishers, 2004), 22.

p. 65,    "by any means…" Anthony A. Williams and Kevin P. Chavous, "Education, By Any Means." *The Washington Post,* April 14, 2009, News section.

p. 68,    "Kennedy represented…" Lewis, *Walking with the Wind,* 239.

p. 70,    "will face…" Ibid., 251.

p. 72,    "[I would] to some little…" Ibid., 262.

p. 73,    "If you seat…" Nick Kotz, *Judgment Days: Lyndon Baines Johnson, Martin Luther King, and the Laws that Changed America,* (Boston: Houghton Mifflin, 2005), 191.

p. 74,    "if the Freedom Democratic Party…" "Racial Voting Rights in America," *The National Park Service: U.S. Department of the Interior Register of Historic Places*, http://www.nps.gov/nhl/Themes/Voting%20Rights%20Theme%20Study.pdf.

p. 74,    "That was…" Lewis, *Walking with the Wind,* 266.

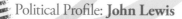 

# Sources *(continued)*

## Chapter Five: Dark Days

p. 83,   "I don't know how…" Lewis, *Walking with the Wind,* 330.

p. 83,   "This was a…" Ibid., 331.

p. 85,   "Rarely in any…" "Special Message to the
Congress: The American Promise," *Lyndon Baines Johnson
Library and Museum,* http://www.lbjlib.utexas.edu/johnson/
archives.hom/speeches.hom/6503.

p. 88,   "There was never…" Hill, *John Lewis,* 81.

p. 89,   "As I rode…" Lewis, *Walking with the Wind,* 374.

p. 90,   "the black American…" Graves, *I Have a Dream: The Story
Behind Martin Luther King Jr.'s Most Famous Speech,* 26.

p. 92,   "But the vast…" ``Statement on the Assassination of Martin
Luther King," *The John F. Kennedy Presidential Library and
Museum,* http://www.jfklibrary.org/Historical+Resources/
Archives/Reference+Desk/Speeches/RFK/Statement+on+the
+Assassination+of+Martin+Luther+King.html.

p. 92,   "Dr. King was…" Lewis, *Walking with the Wind,* 392.

p. 92,   "made me who…" Hill, *John Lewis,* 87.

p. 94,   "We lost something…" Ibid., 88.

p. 94,   "The sense of…" Lewis, *Walking with the Wind,* 401.

## Chapter Six: A New Path

p. 101,   "cool poet…" Lewis, *Walking with the Wind,* 439.

p. 102,   "John Lewis is…" Ibid., 445.

p. 103,   "I thought…" Ibid., 454.

p. 104,   "Freedom Train…" Hill, *John Lewis,* 102.

## Chapter Seven: The Beloved Community

p. 106,   "I've seen courage…" "Meet John Lewis," *John Lewis for
Congress,* www.johnlewisforcongress.com.

p. 108,   "friendship and support…" Ibid., 107.

p. 110,   "Dr. King…" Ibid., 108.

p. 114,   "People have been…" Remnick, "The President's Hero."

p. 116,   "Barack Obama is…" Ibid.

p. 117,   "Children holding hands…" Lewis, *Walking with the Wind,* 13.

# Bibliography

Bausum, Ann. *Freedom Riders: John Lewis and Jim Zwerg on the Front Lines of the Civil Rights Movement.* Washington: National Geographic, 2006.

Coller, Andie. "A 'Down Payment on the Dream.'" *John Lewis for Congress,* January 20, 2009, http://www.johnlewisforcongress.com/node/232.

"Congressman John Lewis (D-GA) Tells NPR News His 2008 Presidential Endorsement Options Between Senators Clinton and Obama are a 'Tough Decision." *NPR.org,* March 30, 2007, http://www.npr.org/about/press/2007/033007.lewis.html.

Evans, Ben. Associated Press. "Segregationist Who Beat John Lewis Asks Forgiveness." *John Lewis for Congress,* February 5, 2009, http://www.johnlewisforcongress.com/node/248.

Graves, Kerry A. *I Have a Dream: The Story Behind Martin Luther King Jr.'s Most Famous Speech.* Philadelphia: Chelsea Clubhouse, 2004.

Hansen, Drew D. *The Dream: Martin Luther King, Jr. and the Speech that Inspired a Nation.* New York: HarperCollins, 2003.

Haskins, Jim, and Kathleen Benson. *John Lewis in the Lead: A Story of the Civil Rights Movement.* New York: Lee & Low Books, 2006.

Hill, Christine. *John Lewis: From Freedom Rider to Congressman.* Berkeley Heights, NJ: Enslow Publishers, 2002.

John F. Kennedy Presidential Library and Museum. http://www.jfklibrary.org/Historical+Resources/Archives/Reference+Desk/Speeches/RFK/Statement+on+the+Assassination+of+Martin+Luther+King.html.

John Lewis official Congressional Web site. http://www.johnlewis.house.gov.

Jones, Clarence B., and Joel Engel. *What Would Martin Say?* New York: HarperCollins, 2008.

Kotz, Nick. *Judgment Days: Lyndon Baines Johnson, Martin Luther King, and the Laws that Changed America.* Boston: Houghton Mifflin, 2005.

Lewis, John. *Walking with the Wind: A Memoir of the Movement.* New York: Simon & Schuster, 1998.

Lyndon Baines Johnson Library and Museum. http://www.lbjlib.utexas.edu/johnson/archives.hom/speeches.hom/6503.

Martin Luther King Research and Education Institute. http://www.mlk-kpp01.stanford.edu/index.php/kingpapers/article/freedom_rides.

# Bibliography *(continued)*

National Park Service: U.S. Department of the Interior Register of Historic Places. http://www.nps.gov/nhl/Themes/Voting%20 Rights%20Theme%20Study.pdf.

Powledge, Fred. *We Shall Overcome: Heroes of the Civil Rights Movement.* New York: Charles Scribner's Sons, 1993.

Remnick, David. "The President's Hero." *New Yorker,* February 2, 2009, http://www.newyorker.com.

U.S. Equal Employment Opportunity Commission. http://www.eeoc.gov/about/eeoc/35th/pre1965/index.html.

Wade, Wyn Craig. *The Ku Klux Klan in America: The Fiery Cross.* New York: Oxford University Press, 1987.

Williams, Anthony A., and Kevin P. Chavous. "Education, By Any Means." *Washington Post,* April 14, 2009.

# Web Sites

**http://www.johnlewis.house.gov**
This is John Lewis's official Web site as a U.S. representative from Georgia. It includes pertinent information about him, his policies, his speeches, upcoming issues, latest news, photos, constituent services, press releases, and contact information for his offices.

**http://www.johnlewisforcongress.com**
This is Lewis's official campaign Web site. Here you'll find his biography, his views, news updates, press releases, photos of different events, and speeches.

**http://www.voicesofcivilrights.org**
The AARP, the Leadership Conference on Civil Rights (LCCR), and the Library of Congress teamed up to collect thousands of personal stories of the civil rights movement. Read these vivid stories, listen to oral accounts, and watch videos about civil rights pioneers of the past and today.

# Index

# Photo Credits

Cover image: Courtesy United States Congress.
2: AP Images/Ric Feld
5: Private Collection
8: Library of Congress
10: AP Images
11: AP Images
13: Library of Congress
16: Library of Congress
20: Library of Congress
21: Courtesy Congressman John Lewis
23: Stan Wayman/Time Life Pictures/Getty Images
24: Library of Congress
26: Library of Congress
27: Library of Congress
28: Library of Congress
30: National Archives and Records Administration/ U.S. Information Agency
33: Private Collection
35: Private Collection
36: Library of Congress
37: Library of Congress
45: Library of Congress
48: Library of Congress
53: AP Images/Horace Cort
58: AP Images

59: AP Images/Bill Hudson
60: Private Collection
62: National Archives
64: National Archives
66: AP Images
69: Library of Congress
73: Will D. Campbell Papers, McCain Library & Archives, University of Southern Mississippi
75: Library of Congress
79: National Atlas
80: AP Images/Bill Hudson
82: AP Images
84: Library of Congress; bottom photo Courtesy AP Images
86: AP Images
88: Library of Congress
93: Private Collection
99: Lewis family photo Courtesy John Lewis; Jimmy Carter Courtesy Private Collection
103: AP Photo/Ric Feld
104: AP Photo/Linda Schaeffer
109: AP Photo/John Duricka
111: AP Photo/Charles Pereira/U.S. Park Service
115: AP Photo/John Amis
117: AP Photo/Andy Amis

Book cover and interior design by Derrick Carroll of DC Designs.